FORMAL COUNTRY

FORMAL COUNTRY

PAT ROSS

Photographs by DAVID PHELPS

Design by LEONARD TODD

FRIEDMAN/FAIRFAX
PUBLISHERS

Books By Pat Ross:

Decorating Your Garden:
An Inspired Look at Ornamental Objects & Furnishings

The Country Cupboard: Kitchens

The Country Cupboard: Flowers

The Country Cupboard: Herbs

Please Come For Dinner

Formal Country Entertaining

To Have & To Hold: Decorative American Boxes

A Perfect Cup Of Tea

Remembering Main Street: An American Album

A FRIEDMAN/FAIRFAX BOOK

Text © copyright 1989, 1999 by PKR Concepts, Inc.
Photographs © copyright 1989, 1999 by David Phelps

Library of Congress Cataloging-in-Publication data available upon request.

ISBN 1-56799-948-4

Printed in Hong Kong by Dai Nippon Printing Co Ltd

3 5 7 9 10 8 6 4 2

For bulk purchases and special sales, please contact:
Friedman/Fairfax Publishers
Attention: Sales Department
15 West 26th Street
New York, New York 10010
212/685-6610   FAX 212/685-1307

Visit our website:
www.metrobooks.com

For Jerri Fowler,
loving aunt & childhood inspiration.

—*P. R.*

To my parents,
Dean and Jean Phelps.

—*D. P.*

CONTENTS

ACKNOWLEDGMENTS

We are indebted to the many wonderful people who allowed us into their homes, made room for the many cases of camera equipment, and put up with the invasion of their privacy during the shooting of this book. To those who allowed us to use their names along with their stories, and to those who wished to retain their privacy in print—our sincere thanks!

At the top of my list is Patricia O'Shaughnessy, who acted as scout and prop stylist for a number of locations in this book. She divided herself into manager, stylist, and designer, and pulled it off in a style that is uniquely her own.

Locations such as the ones we found are not uncovered without a great deal of networking and detective work. Our networks were made possible by Leah Sklar, Amala and Eric Levine, Jinny Clark, Karla Waterman, Ingrid Savage, Diane Glenn, Robert and Barbara Story, Leo Kelmenson, Patricia Lovejoy, Meri Stevens, Ann Bigelow, Bill and Mary McGrail, William and Kathleen Doyle, Wendy Nelson, Melody Fleckenstein, Haje O'Neil, and Roberta Sherman.

So many designers, dealers, and style writers flipped through their Rolodexes and invested generous portions of their personal time to help. We are grateful to Nancy Wing and Anne Leonard who get four stars each; Kim Freeman for an early welcome; Allison Percival of *House Beautiful* for her generosity of spirit; Kathy Schoemer for our country visit;

Susan Lyle for her support; D. J. Carey of *1001 Decorating Ideas* for her good ideas; Linda Humphrey for helping make Seattle a reality; Paula Perlini and Susan Anthony for contributing their design styles; Stan Hura for his helpful ways.

The Museum of American Folk Art, New York, is a constant source of inspiration and support. Thank you, Lucy and Mike Danziger, for appreciating the scope of the projects and making your expertise available to us; Marie DiManno, for your cheerful enthusiasm; and Didi Barrett, for your support and the tour.

There is really no way to adequately acknowledge the energetic and supportive staff at Sweet Nellie for their willingness to keep the show on the road during my necessary absences. Sincere appreciation to Beth Tudor for calmly keeping all the details of both the business and the book straight and putting everything on the computer. It's reassuring to know that all of you are just offstage: Arlene Kirkwood, Marie-Nicole Elian, and Amy LaLone especially. David Phelps and I appreciated the support of Michael Kane and Mark Hill.

Leisa Crane does research more thoroughly than anyone I know. Thank you to Leisa for making the book's Resources section a shopper's delight, and to Heather Connors for updating it for the 10th anniversary edition.

Many shops felt a special kinship with this project and were happy to loan their ideas as well as their merchandise: Beth Alberg at Random Harvest; our neighboring shops Ronaldo Maia and Eric Landgraf, Florist; Sandy Washburn at The Cottage at Chappaqua; the helpful staff at Charlotte Moss Antiques; Louise Arnold and Corky Andrews at Arnold and Andrews; Geri Williams and Janet Lynch at The Golden Swan, Michele Clise at Bazaar des Bears; Patricia Tall and B. J. Harris at Panache; Jane Rivkin at Kitchen Classics, who put up with all the UPS; Fishers Antiques; Balasses Antiques; Diana Berkowitz and Alyne Schwartz at Richard's Interiors; and Ron Schwartz at Treganowan for kindly loaning us the hooked rug on page 109.

A special debt of gratitude to the artisans who were rarely too busy to make up special orders for us to use in the book: Liz Lawrence, Daniel Mack, Gail Peachin, Ivan Barnett, Barbara Eigen, and Arabelle Taggart. Our appreciation to all the talented artisans we know—we wish it had been possible to include each one of you in these pages.

One can never have too many friends during the months that an idea is becoming a reality. Barry Yaker, your wonderful Aspen home turned work into a vacation! For heart-felt support and message units freely given, I thank you all: Nancy Kruger, Kate Williams, Judy Crawford, Carolyn Gore, Pat Upton, Laurel and Patricia Doody (my Seattle support crew), Margie and Tom Haber, Frank Ockenfels, Jan Arnow, Conrad and Linda Foa, and Amy Berkower at Writer's House.

The unreserved and unqualified support of family is necessary to landing on your feet when the deadline rolls around. Always there for me are Anita Kienzle, Jeanne Kienzle, and Erica Ross.

A man of many talents, Leonard Todd has taken our words and our images and combined them in a splendid design that perfectly expresses our ideas. My appreciation goes to him for investing so much of himself in this book.

For the first edition of this book, Michael Fragnito and Barbara Williams at Viking Studio Books generated sufficient talent and support to keep it going for a decade. For the 10th Anniversary edition, I'd like to thank the energetic team at Michael Friedman Publishing, including Michael Friedman, Bruce Lubin, Sharyn Rosart, and Jeff Batzli for the lovely new jacket design. Last, but not least, thanks to Denise McGann for encouraging an encore.

Foreword to the 10th Anniversary Edition

As we made plans to bring out the 10th Anniversary Edition of *Formal Country*, my publisher asked if there were revisions I wished to make. Any writer will tell you that getting a second chance like this is a rare gift. For a tireless *redecorator* like me, it was much like being given permission to strip off the too-bold wallpaper I'd adored at the time, replace Aunt Rosie's old chair with something a bit less ungainly, or rearrange all my closets at once. I couldn't wait. I began to thumb through my book in search of ideas that may have gathered decorating dust bunnies over the past decade. Immediately, the resources section sprang to mind. Otherwise, I was, uncharacteristically, speechless.

When *Formal Country* was first published in 1989, this new design concept—combining classic stylishness with good old-fashioned country charm—was for many a rebellious notion. (I recall that it took courage for one of my friends to place a treasured Shaker box, its original paint softly weathered, on a highly polished Chippendale table.) I admit to my share of weak impulses, especially when I spot trendy and enticing spreads in glossy design magazines or tour perfectly appointed rooms at the latest decorator showhouse. I've skipped down that path before, finding myself temporarily stuck with hot colors that jar, monochromatic color schemes that are too serene for my personality, an "antique" beanbag chair that reminded me too much of my adolescence, and a blowzy slipcover that looked like the dress *after* the crash diet. Although I've given both our city apartment and place in the country their share of irrepressible decorating re-dos, I always come back to combining the easy warmth of country style with the elegance of classic good taste. It suits me best.

A decade after the book's publication, Formal Country means much the same in design terms, but its possibilities have expanded to include even more eclectic elements—styles, colors, and cultural influences—and a sense of spontaneity. French and English country styles—always such strong inspirations in East Coast homes and in my book—were experiencing a westward migration when *Formal Country* was published. At the same time, the Pacific's own rich style history, with its vibrant colors and unmistakable spirit, was making itself felt in the East. With the high-living Eighties came an excess of baroque, which never worked for me, even though once I tried my hand at gilding a humble bathroom to death. I was grateful for a breath of fresh air in the Nineties, with beautiful woods and slim lines coming to the fore. Neverthelss, over the years, as historical influences were reworked and refreshed, our choices for true eclecticism were expanding. (However, I would like to think that the raked shag rug of the Sixties will never return.)

Soon after *Formal Country* was published, the Arts & Crafts movement began to receive a long overdue share of attention. Back in 1989, my own experience with the straightforward lines and fine craftsmanship of Mission style was limited to what I read in books on design history. Today, several rooms of our farmhouse in Virginia have been given a new dimension with the design strength of Stickley. So, if I had it to do over again at the beginning of a new century, would I do things differently? Inevitably, one learns a few things in ten years. However, it's gratifying to know that the design premise remains much the same. In that respect, I would not change a thing.

Much to my delight, the resurgence of interest in the American crafts tradition—a passion that inspired me to open Sweet Nellie in 1983 and sell only things handcrafted and American—has been a lasting one. The "cute" country craft shop has gone more upscale, more savvy in its ability to make craft synonymous with fine design. From folk and whimsical to high style and contemporary, handcrafted furniture and objects have found their way into our eclectic design language. I'd like to think that *Formal Country* was on the cutting edge of this thinking.

Other styles have come and gone—much like my pretentious short-lived draperies that puddled—while the design lexicon I christened "formal country" has grown steadily in popularity. For everyone who's found a kindred spirit in these ideas and in the stunning photography of David Phelps, *Formal Country* is back for a curtain call.

—Pat Ross

INTRODUCTION

The title of this book—*Formal Country*—may at first seem like a puzzling contradiction. "Formal" has traditionally suggested elegant interiors filled with period antiques and dramatic flourishes; "country" has come to mean more relaxed and accessible rooms filled to overflowing with primitive pieces and cheerful rustic touches. When these two decorating styles—formal and country—work together, as they do in this book, the contradiction of the title soon disappears, providing new possibilities for a life-style that celebrates the elegance of formal and the warmth of country under the same roof. So whether one calls the resulting style Formal Country, Sophisticated Country, Relaxed Formal, or even High Country, the apparent clash of two styles has made way for a winning style different from either.

Breaking the rules and mixing country with other styles of decorating has gained popularity only in the relatively recent past. Over the years, country decorating has been a category unto itself. The definition of country gradually broadened and stretched until a wider acceptance of its qualities took hold. It is interesting to look back over the years and see just how far country decorating has come.

Growing up in the forties and fifties, I can remember a stack of *Better Homes & Gardens* on our coffee table, and I have vivid memories of my mother clipping from them. The magazine showed to the American public a country decorating style that was pleasantly old-fashioned and comfortably cozy. In our house, wallpapers in diminutive prints that my mother called "provincials" covered miles of kitchen, hallways, and bedrooms. Our kitchen curtains were trimmed in ball fringe, usually red

and cheerful. I had an overdose of ball fringe back then, along with ruffled tie-backs, and to this day I resist using curtains, draperies, or ball fringe of any kind!

The country style of that day favored somber machine-braided rugs and admirable furniture reproductions. Hitchcock rockers and chairs were reproduced by well-known furniture makers in quanitity. The style was often fussy and overdone, but at the same time there was something comforting about a home like that.

A fresher, more fashionable American country style emerged in the mid-sixties in *House & Garden*, when the designer Sister Parish of the renowned Parish-Hadley firm decorated her own home in Maine with country oak furniture that she painted white. The story goes that Sister Parish had purchased over a hundred oak pieces at a country barn sale and set about painting and placing them on painted floors and handwoven rugs. The more formal accessories that she is best known for—the luxu-rious chintzes, the fine needlework pieces, the dog paintings—were all incorporated into a divergent country look, giving it a sense of enormous elegance and panache.

The seventies was a time of flowering for country decorating. Mary Emmerling's style books on American country treated an enthusiastic public to the best of primitive folk art, cherished textiles, and original painted finishes on rustic furniture. For a touch of the French countryside, Pierre Deux offered cheerful fabric designs that were immediately recognizable. Laura Ashley brought the English country look into closer focus, while Ralph Lauren added his American-style chic. Countless other shops and companies specializing in a universal range of country items sprang up throughout the United States. Suddenly, the choices seemed unlimited.

During the conception, photographing, and, finally, the writing of *Formal Country*, I thought

mostly about the customers at my Madison Avenue shop, Sweet Nellie. It seemed that customers with more formal tastes sought out unusual folk art, pretty painted pottery, and more rustic hand-crafted accessories to soften their settings. Customers with country homes and country tastes brought a needed sophistication to their settings with the graceful formal touches that an elegant needlepoint pillow or a striking paisley throw could provide.

I have seen photographs of my customers' city apartments and country homes in various stages of renovating and redecorating, worked with their paint chips and fabric swatches, and pored over their clipping files. And so I kept recalling their enthusastic questions about the various decorative objects old and new that I sell in my shop: Who is the artisan? What is the medium? How old is the piece? Where is it from? Is it signed and dated? I also thought about my customers' eagerness to mix styles and take chances with design combinations. It's this sense of personal expression and pride that

encouraged me to seek out homes for this book whose owners had interpreted Formal Country in fresh and special ways, resulting in new ideas for all of us.

Formal Country means a new freedom to approach interior arrangements and combine decorating styles. In seeking locations for *Formal Country*, we were treated to an exciting and eclectic mix: the old and the new, originals and reproductions, formal and informal. Folk art coexisted with fine art, crafted objects flattered period pieces; the mismatched became unique, not odd; unexpected juxtapositions were dramatic revelations. We found a soapbox racer from the twenties in an elegant living room, an elebarate silver service on a rustic table, southwestern pottery next to Chippendale. Possible conflicts became admirable contrasts. Suddenly, people were writing this book for us by sharing their expressive ideas and personal styles.

This book admits to a bias for the many wonderful details that make up the total look. Pottery—

in collections as well as interesting single pieces—became a rich common denominator throughout. We found decorative boxes in all shapes and sizes, made of wood, paper, and cloth. There were pretty hatboxes newly made and painted boxes with impressive histories. The folk art treasures were often whimsical, thoroughly original, and always well placed. Many of the rugs were handwoven because the owners could not find what they wanted in a machine-made rug. Baskets held flowers, fruit, and vegetables, when they did not stand empty for the sole purpose of admiration. Pieces of treasured old textiles were made into pillows and seat cushions, or used as table covers. We sought out the most picture-perfect arrangements—from the most spare groupings to the most exuberant, organized clutter. Happily, there seemed no end to the imaginative displays of antique and newly made decorative objects.

We were fortunate to be able to photograph many of the locations of this book during the spring and summer months, when flower gardens were full and beautiful. In looking back, it seems more than coincidental that most of the people who graciously opened their homes to us also turned us loose with garden shears and gave us free run of the blooms and greens in their city backyards and country gardens. We were treated to an abundance of cheerful daisies, dew-drenched hydrangeas, sassy zinnias, blossoming peonies, and lilies of breathtaking lemon yellow and tiger orange. Wild roses and flowering vines found their way to dressing tables and dining room tables. Not surprisingly, there was never a lack of an interesting vase or display piece that doubled as a container for the garden array.

In the fall, our arrangements shifted to include a variety of greens, berries, flowers, and leaves in autumnal hues. We were treated to bountiful fresh garden vegetables when the occasion called for it. When we needed to supplement an arrangement, country markets offered a hearty selection of the lushest, most photogenic fare anyone could ask for.

The garden details of *Formal Country* soon became a natural and essential part of the book.

We felt like special guests and old friends in many of the homes we photographed. One cheerful and welcoming homeowner prepared such a delicious and picture-perfect lunch for us that we photographed it (quickly!) before sitting down to enjoy it. A pot of fresh-brewed coffee left out for us kept us going during many ten-hour days.

Wherever we went, we found the joyful marriage of the old and the new, antique and craft. American craft has come a long way since the quilted chicken toaster cover, the teddy bear carving board, and the universal brown coffee mug. Adjectives such as "cute" and "quaint" need no longer apply to the work of an amazing diversity of artisans whose talent and sophistication blur the line between art and craft. Today's traditional decorative accessories include the best of one-of-a-kind details for every room of the house and the garden. The addition of a handwoven rug, a wreath of dried flowers, or a marbleized picture frame can mean that interiors take on a personality and unique charm that is impossible to duplicate with mass-market production.

It would be a terrible oversight to neglect to include the names of the artisans whose work has given creative energy to the decorative arts movement today. We were delighted to find homeowners proudly naming crafts people whose work graced their homes. Since most of these artisans are living and working today, many people decorate with the thought of collecting and commissioning as well. Whenever possible, we have credited artisans with their handcrafts and we apologize for anyone who may inadvertently remain unsung in these pages.

What we hope we've arrived at in *Formal Country* is an *interpretation* of a style, not a dictionary definition. If the resulting "film clips" of people's lives, along with the recounting of their creativity and personal styles, provide fresh ideas, then we are happy to have found and shared them.

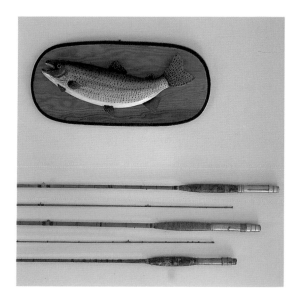

Predominantly Formal

TRULY TOWN
AND COUNTRY

It is easy to forget that this town house sits nestled among so many other houses and high-rises in the middle of Manhattan. If it offers solace and serenity from the world outside, it is not by sheer chance. The owners—a retired British lawyer who's hard at work on a novel about the financial world and a German-born professor of philosophy whose special area of interest is Existentialism—set out to create a haven for themselves and their family. "Privacy" and "peacefulness" are words that come up frequently in a conversation about the house and its interior.

Four years ago, when this couple met and married after a whirlwind courtship, they decided to begin a new life with each other and take a fresh look at their environment. Forsaking past styles and many belongings that no longer held meaning for them, they eagerly embraced the renovation and decoration of their late-nineteenth-century town house, hoping to bring together their shared interests in things formal and European with an affection for the warmth and charm that newly crafted objects could bring. The result is a mix that can be described as tastefully understated and brimming with softness and light, a seemingly effortless project.

Flowers are considered an important part of their lives and part of their decorating taste. Every Tuesday morning, well before breakfast, the two set out for New York's flower district, where they select

Left: The tone of this late-nineteenth-century town house is one of restrained formality. Country touches, such as painted pottery and decorative boxes, add warmth and interest.

Left: Peonies, the first of the season, seem to burst from their cachepot. The newly crafted bronze birds were discovered in Italy. They sit on the eighteenth-century French marble mantel.

flowers for that week's arrangements, which practically spill from every room. Part of the Tuesday morning ritual includes breakfast after the flower shopping at one of the downtown coffee shops, then home to arrange the armfuls of plants and fresh-cut flowers.

Floral motifs are echoed in the fabrics and accessories. Handcrafted bowls and pitchers, frames and boxes are decorated with soft flower designs. Potted plants from the carefully planned and pruned garden off the dining room find their way into bowls and baskets.

With the week's flowers placed about, the house is ready to offer the serenity and natural beauty needed by two people who live and work best when surrounded by the things they love. Strains of Mozart and Vivaldi complete the picture of a European refuge in the middle of Manhattan.

*Above: The hand-painted box
by Charles Muise and two
earth-tone pitchers by Judy
Kogod add interest to the sideboard when it is not laden
with buffets for the many
guests who visit.*

*Left: The warm wood tones of
the dining room, done mostly
with English and French
country antiques, provide the
background for newly crafted
ceramics, decorative and
functional.*

Right: The doors on this French cupboard were removed and installed in reverse so that they would openly invite guests to admire the collection of blueware and silver.

Below: The dried wreath is from Cherchez, a charming shop that is, happily, just a few blocks away.

Above: The hydrangeas on Judy Kogod's pretty platter keep company with their real counterparts, dried and saved from the year before.

Above: Old fabric-covered frames hold family memories.

Left: A handwoven throw by Kathy Evans provides warmth, both physical and decorative. Vintage wallpaper boxes by Berta Montgomery become a novel end table.

Above: Various floral motifs— seen here on pottery by Maddy Fraioli and in a framed nineteenth-century water-color—are an extension of the owners' desire to be sur- rounded by flowers, both decorative and real-life.

9

Right: Grace and elegance are found in a pocket-size backyard garden in the middle of Manhattan. The French limestone horses date from the nineteenth century.

Above: Liz Lawrence paints delicate Matisse-like room scenes—which appear to mimic the architectural details of the larger setting—on ceramics, such as this lamp and bowl.

FOLKTALE INSPIRED

The temperature dips dramatically as visitors turn off a major Washington state highway and wind through local roads toward a densely wooded area near the coast. Beneath ancient fir trees whose needles make paths soft and pungent, a grand chalet-style house looks as though it has been there forever, which was the intention of the owners. Guests cannot dispel the impression that they may have wandered into a Bavarian folktale centuries old.

Long before any plan for their dream house had been put down on paper, the homeowners snapped up a number of magnificent old doors from a local architectural salvage company and put them in storage. The doors, which had been brought over from Belgium, included pristine French doors with etched and frosted glass panels, a massive arched door of weathered oak, and a set of sliding barn doors with the original paint untouched. These doors brought back fond memories for the owners of extended stays in Germany and return trips to visit old friends. When the couple finally built their Swiss-inspired house, the resulting architectual design and interior decorating style brought together all the things they had for so long loved and admired.

The owners took a confident but lighthearted approach to the way the interiors would be treated. Their family furniture—mostly fine heirlooms—suddenly seemed too formal, but the couple would never dream of replacing it. They chose instead to add country-style touches—according to their European taste, of course—to relax the formal atmosphere and provide warmth and charm. Rich and mellow, their color palette became reminiscent of

Left: The owners decided to turn a cozy area off the kitchen, originally planned as a laundry room, into a useful larder and to move the laundry out of sight.

Left: You almost expect elves from the forest to step right into these authentic Dutch shoes, collected—and worn—in all sizes by the owners over many years.

Brueghel and Hals. Accessories seem to have been plucked from a Grimm fairy tale: a timeworn porcelain goose, three colorful bisque hens, an odd arrangement of wooden shoes. Guests are tempted to look under the old stencil-painted bed for an elf or a gnome. Outside, the sheltering forest shades every room and provides the only window treatment the owners need.

There are paths that wind from the yard into the wooded area beyond. One path leads past a decorative bird feeder to the gazebo, where all three generations of the family often bring their lunch. Another path leads right to a pair of willow chairs that appear carefully positioned in the sunniest spot. On lazy holidays, the family plays croquet through the needle-covered paths. And when the grandchildren grow weary, it's time for a story—a folktale, no doubt. . . .

14

Above: The stone wall planter, one of a pair used in the foyer, was made in Italy, a facsimile of a piece from antiquity.

Left: The hand-painted Italian tiles were leftovers from a shop that custom-makes tile stoves. The tin cow sculpture is a folk art reproduction.

Above: The French porcelain goose is over two hundred years old and is speckled with the many hairline fractures of age.

Left: The French pine cupboard and formal dining-room table and chairs work well together. The room can go from formal to informal with a simple change of table linens and dishes.

Right: The three original sitting hens in the cupboard were bought on three separate trips to Germany. The vendor's cart, an old one, holds a merry mix of plants.

Above: A setting for guests with the Sunday best includes the family's Wedgwood china and Waterford crystal. The colorful artificial fruit nosegays are from the 1930s, probably picked up in a then-ubiquitous five-and-ten. Here they make festive napkin rings.

Above: The local artisan John Calvo recently hand stenciled the old family wedding bed. The owners gave Calvo total freedom with his design and were delighted with the result.

Above: A bolder version of the bed's floral design was chosen for the floor of the room.

Left: The view to the woods beyond is never interrupted by curtains or shades.

Left: The window used to be part of a spice shop in the old Seattle Pike's Place Market and was rescued during demolition some years ago. The elegant French tub is nickel on copper and teakwood. What appears in the background to be a deer-motif pillow is actually an exceptionally beautiful silk scarf wrapped around a pillow.

Above: Sunlight through the trees warms the wash stand.

21

Left: Frosted and etched glass doors from Belgium open onto a patio off the foyer.

Below: The iron Empire-style chair is new; the pedestal was a local antique-shop find.

Below right: The owners collect canes that strike their fancy, old and new, and they use them for walks in the woods. The brass stand is generous in size so there's room for the collection to expand.

Above: The patio is cool and restful, sheltered by the many trees, and is used for light meals and respites from gardening.

23

Left: The many exquisite doors throughout this grand chalet-style house were sought out from architectural salvage companies years before any design was put on paper. Here, a door from Belgium is decorated with grapevine, wild blackberries, and wild strawberry vines from the dense woods beyond.

Above and below left: The rustic willow is right at home!

Right: The family often picnics in the gazebo and plays a tricky game of croquet through the forest paths.

A COUNTRY GENTLEMAN'S RETREAT

Someone else's home becomes yours, if only for the length of the job, when you are given the task of selecting furnishings and decorative accessories that reflect that someone else's tastes. Paula Perlini faced this delicate challenge as the designer for a successful advertising executive, a man whose busy public life left little time for coordinating all the details that were a necessary part of renovating and redecorating his weekend retreat. Mark Hampton, a designer whose exquisite sense of the social traditions of the past has earned him high praise and respect, has, since he started his own business, designed every home for this client, and Paula Perlini was project man-

ager on each job.

It was clear to Perlini from the start that the client's overwhelming interest in things nautical would figure prominently into the decorating plan. A world traveler, he collects a judicious variety of seafaring treasures—from authentic trade signs to quirky salvage finds. Perlini soon grew accustomed to finding the right place for each and every piece, down to the last rope, dowel, and anchor.

Perlini knew that the client was a very private person whose weekends were an essential buffer against his hectic professional week. An involved homeowner, he needed an elegant yet comfortable decor that wouldn't show boot tracks or paw prints. He wanted the kind of comfortable atmosphere that

Left: The hunt is the theme of the game room, which offers country comfort in a tradition- ally formal setting.

Left: The riding tack and related gear, casually arranged on the side table, are for admiration rather than use.

makes everyone feel welcome. The intimate dining room was planned for small gatherings, with most meals becoming a joyful group effort.

Perlini did her homework, and she obviously did her job to perfection. The comfortable give-and-take working relationship has resulted in yet more projects for this designer and client who seem to understand each other.

Above: In the dining room and throughout the house, English country furniture, antique botanicals, and deep colors set the tone for the busy owner's weekend retreats.

Left: Candles in mismatching holders create a play of light.

Far left: The hearty old seaman who created these knots would never have dreamed that they would one day be arranged behind glass. The fine antique sled propped against the wall is an interesting way to handle a special memory from the past.

29

Left: Because the house is near the water, the telescope is used for more than just decoration. The model boat is just one of many nautical objects favored by the home-owner, who enjoys sailing his own boat, which is often docked within view.

Below: Once again, the recurring nautical theme of the house is seen in the owner's love for folk art and objects from the sea. A clever head-board design has been fashioned from a sailing sign and an architectural detail.

Below right: It seems that all things blue and white, the proverbial favorite country color combination, go together. This holds true of the Kentucky Derby poster, a signed Peter Max, and the old basin set in the guest bedroom.

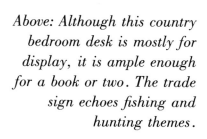

Above: Although this country bedroom desk is mostly for display, it is ample enough for a book or two. The trade sign echoes fishing and hunting themes.

SOPHISTICATED
COUNTRY

NORTHWESTERN GRACE

Everything about this Bainbridge Island house overlooking a broad expanse of Puget Sound toward Seattle says "made in Washington." Visitors are greeted by a Betz Bernhard garden sculpture, an affectionate-looking lamb constructed of concrete and fiberglass and commissioned by the present owners along with a two-hundred-and-fifty-pound concrete pig, who is permanently settled in the backyard. Natural state resources, such as the Snohomish River rock used in the construction of the fireplace, were sought out and incorporated into the architectural details of a property that has experienced a renaissance.

The present house—a sprawling traditional design with contemporary accents of expansive glass —is a far cry from the plain 1920s summer cottage that once occupied the site, which was chosen by

its new owners primarily for its majestic location overlooking the Sound. They were also delighted to discover that the land was covered with a wealth of untended foliage and flowers, including more than a hundred different species of rhododendron indigenous to the area. With the help of landscape specialists and the area's talented craftsmen, the property was developed into a spacious family home with an enviable garden.

Room after room is filled, but never crowded, with work by Washington's artists and artisans, many from Bainbridge Island. One of the owners of this house is recognized in the community for her wonderfully creative flower arrangements done in unique baskets. Throughout the house, hand-crafted objects are mixed with a selection of country antiques and showcased against walls painted dramatic shades of purple and green. The own-

Left: The graceful lines of an old buggy seat stand out in a spare and uncluttered setting. The still life above is by Roslyn Gale Powell.

Left: The family uses the weathered trunk to store old shoes, boots, and children's games. The decoy on top was carved by Bob Stone of Montana.

ers wanted a sophisticated setting where decorative objects could be admired without distraction. Bleached floors add to the feeling of simplicity. The resulting look is bold and confident.

An intense loyalty to local artisans has not prevented the owners from seeking out folk art and crafts from other parts of the globe. Vacations to Mexico frequently turn into shopping sprees. Because the owners are attracted to "surfaces with character," they sought out old church doors and had them made into massive tables. They delight in the way primitive wood plays against their smooth marbleized walls and bold color scheme.

Long-time patrons of the arts, these people believe that the inclusion of handcrafted objects brings warmth and sensitivity to their home, offering a spontaneity, subtlety, and richness that mass-produced items could never approach. They feel that a well-chosen object reflects the personality of its maker and adds life to a setting.

Above: The primitive wooden horse from a midwestern antiques dealer was actually used by the owners' three sons when they were children, so it has withstood much devotion over the years.

Left: This homeowner's flair for display is apparent throughout her northwestern home, especially in the hallway, where she has artfully draped a Peruvian rug over a Mexican tabletop and then placed a basket of colorful papiermâché vegetables at a tilt on the floor.

37

Left: The rough-hewn and the well-polished complement each other in a consistent decorating theme that runs throughout the rooms of this house. Here, the rustic Mexican table (which used to be a door) and chairs contrast with the sleek glazed walls. The flower designers Blooming on Bainbridge arranged fresh-cut flowers in a hemp basket for a dramatic accent.

Right: Gardening and vegetables are recurring motifs in this pine cupboard. A pitcher by the ceramicist Barbara Eigen, in the shape of fennel (second shelf from bottom on the right), is filled with fresh clipped rosemary from just outside the kitchen door. The sheep butter dish by Suki Diamond (second shelf from top on the left) adds a humorous touch. Most of the pieces were bought at Panache, a downtown Seattle shop favored by the owner.

Above: A basket of ash-tree berries, holly, and a bright orange flower indigenous to Washington state rests prettily on the river rock fireplace.

*Above: A pair of primitive
outdoor chairs was left behind
by the previous owners when
the present house was just a
beach cottage.*

Above: The Seattle artist Betz Bernhard's concrete pig weighs more than two hundred and fifty pounds. It has been given a permanent place of honor just outside the kitchen door.

Right: The noted landscape artist R. David Adams has placed an old field cart among the flower beds he designed.

Below left: One would be hard put to find a sweeter lamb, real or sculpted! This concrete and fiberglass folk piece is by Betz Bernhard.

LIGHT POMP AND CIRCUMSTANCE

The designer Richard Lowell Neas, who has made his gracious and predominantly formal style of decorating available to hundreds of clients, never tires of doing and redoing one home in particular—his own.

The colorful flower boxes set in narrow windows give a strong hint from outside of a European style within. Once inside, guests soon forget that this home is situated on a bluff overlooking the Atlantic and not the Mediterranean, somewhere in the south of France.

Richard Neas, working with his partner, Dennis O'Brien, has lavished touches of French country cheerfully and almost playfully through the house.

An armoire from one of his many trips to the south of France is filled with antique trompe l'oeil objects, colorfully embellished with fruits and vegetables. Since Neas is one of today's most noteworthy artists of trompe l'oeil, it seems fitting for him to have such a splendid collection.

The floors have all been painted by Neas—a comb-painted white design for the living room and, in other rooms, faux stone (*fausse pierre*, I am quickly informed by the expert, is the correct term, though infrequently used), which appears so authentic one must bend down to touch it.

An unexpected surprise is the cool Summer Room. Named for the season, it is always filled with fresh-cut garden flowers and streams of light. This

Left: A corner of the guest bedroom, called the Paisley Room for obvious reasons, is pleasing enough for even the most discerning visitor. The nineteenth-century birdhouse was a carpenter's exercise and can be admired at close range.

Left: A jumble of vines and tendrils threatens to hide the door of a French country treasure trove on the Long Island shore. The main entrance to the house is elsewhere, but visitors prefer this charming mud-room entrance.

overscale room, accessorized with serving-size pieces of delft and faience to match its grandness, is closed off during the bitter winter months, making it all the more special as the year comes full circle again.

Last year, the living room was warmed by soft floral chintz; this year, serene beige curtains and upholstery to match change the appearance of the room completely. The furniture is moved about on a regular basis, as are the many details. Neas and O'Brien have a way of acquiring accessories for one area of the house that very smartly fit a dozen other spots. Happily, there is not a right or a wrong place for anything!

The only American ever asked to decorate a room for the queen of England, Richard Neas shuns pomp and circumstance for his own home. He says he wants his country retreat to be cheerful, comfortable, and informal—a place for guests to be at ease—while retaining a sense of elegance. It is no wonder that this sun-blessed dwelling is so easy to call home.

Above: Organized clutter becomes decoration, and includes stacks of books and magazines on decorating, gardening, architecture, and culinary pleasures.

Left: Richard Neas chose an elegant yet comfortable look for his country cottage, a haven for him, his associate Dennis O'Brien, and their many fortunate guests.

Above and left: A bright and cheerful lineup of delft and faience pieces is displayed on a fausse pierre *mantel and surround, painted by Neas.*

Right: The grand, high-ceilinged Summer Room is open to the rest of the house during the milder seasons only. An overscale statement, it rises to the occasion as a favorite place for dining, reading, or relaxing. All furniture dates from the seventeenth and eighteenth centuries.

Right: The antique fabric for the seventeenth-century armchair was bought from a dealer in Paris.

Above: An eighteenth-century Italian terra-cotta bust, representing one of the four seasons, looks as well placed next to the faience pedestal as on top of it.

Above: The impressive high-back sofa, graced by another Four Seasons bust, is appropriate to the grand scale of the room.

Left: Making a splash with a delft collection.

51

*Below: Dennis O'Brien pre-
pared a lunch that looked
good enough to photograph—
and so we did just that!*

*Above: Neas's enviable collec-
tion of trompe l'oeil fruit and
vegetable objects from Italy,
France, and England fill the
French armoire and work well
with the antique figurines.
Neas relishes creating illu-
sions with decoration and
design, an art that he is
considered a master of.*

Left: Festive weekend occasions are prepared for in a country kitchen that is chock full of antique objects and memorabilia from the south of France. Neas found the nineteenth-century copper molds in a small antiques shop there. The blue trim on the doorway was done by Neas, who painted the other door and window trim to match.

Above: The decorative touches in the small cellar entrance-way—a Canadian Indian basket, French jugs, rustic pots—simply "happened," according to the owners.

Right: The pig above the stove was once an old butcher-shop emblem in France.

ONE-OF-A-KIND SETTING

It is no coincidence that I sell and write about one-of-a-kind decorative objects, both old and new. Growing up in rural Maryland, where county fairs and antiques markets were regular events in our lives, I became familiar with a wealth of crafts and antiques many years ago. It still pleases me to find something for my shop, Sweet Nellie, or for myself that is unique. As a result, my own home—a city apartment with a treetop view of a lovely small park—is filled with many fine handcrafted objects and unusual antiques. I believe that the personality of a talented artisan makes a special difference, and that a treasured antique adds an irreplaceable sense of the past to any setting.

My surroundings have always been important to my peace of mind. After a long day, I need to return to colors, textures, and objects that welcome me and bring to mind fond memories. My formal side is attracted to fine furniture and the luster of old silver. My informal side appreciates timeworn textiles, rustic furniture, and primitive folk art. A Formal Country style means the best of both worlds for me.

Although I thrive on collecting things, I do not consider myself a collector. As a rule, my taste is too eclectic and diverse for me to achieve true collector status. If I am in Santa Fe, I may leave with an Indian rug tucked under my arm; on trips to London, several elaborately trimmed pillows may

Left: Having so many trees just outside my living-room window— and one tree inside— makes our apartment feel more like a country home. I wouldn't dream of hanging curtains, even though I am fond of elegant window treatments.

Left: The pillow maker Arabelle Taggart knew I was looking for blue pillows to go with my new slip covers. When she came across a pair of 1930s draperies at a flea market, she thought of me and made them up as pillows with just-right trim.

cause my luggage to bulge; a trip through New England may find my car filled with old baskets and handwoven blankets. I've learned that by trusting my instincts and color preferences, all the different things I have acquired somehow work together in surprising harmony.

Fortunately, working on *Formal Country* has expanded my interest and given me an abundance of fresh ideas. I discovered decorative Indian clubs, colorful Beacon blankets, and glorious Victorian bird cages, not to mention countless new artisans whose work would add immeasurably to any interior. Unfortunately, I'm running out of space for new discoveries.

Decorating a home is, for me, an endless opportunity to improve the quality of life by bringing into view all the things that make me happy. Our home is not a stage set; it's a place where the dog brings his bedraggled toy onto the sofa and where the rest of us like to relax and enjoy just being together. Elegance is essential, but not without comfort and lighthearted touches. Bringing all these things together is an ongoing source of pleasure.

Above: Our home frequently looks like a box warehouse because of my addiction to collecting them. Fortunately, the various boxes do hold the family's old sweaters, canceled checks, winter gloves, and my teenage daughter's childhood stuffed animals. The old painted cupboard is said to come from Maine.

Left: Berta Montgomery's bandboxes are covered with vintage papers. Boxes such as these have inspired my interest in textile design.

Right: The Maine folk artist Dan Falt calls this aggressive-looking fellow "Killer Pig." I like the contrast between primitive folk-art pieces, old and new, and more refined furniture and accessories, such as the Oriental rug.

Below left and right: The confetti platter designed by ceramicist Lynn Fisher was a gift; the lyrically painted crock, used here as a vase, is by Rhonda Friedman of Maine and is one of many things from my shop that has somehow found its way into my home; the snakes are by the Santa Fe folk carver Jimbo Davila.

Above: When I bought my Lloyd Loom chairs, this furniture was still inexpensive. Now, such vintage porch furniture is next to impossible to find and is rarely inexpensive.

Above: An exquisite beadwork piece—a miniature purse— has been saved for posterity in an antique gold-leaf frame.

Left: A turn-of-the-century Log Cabin quilt becomes abstract art, hung in the hallway above a grain-painted chest.

Above: A morning trip to my neighborhood florist resulted in not one but two bouquets of their most colorful flowers. The angel is my seasonless piece from Daniel Hale; the tea caddy is British; the fish decoy has just been mounted in preparation for its journey to Joel's office, to join his collection of fishing objets.

*Above: Charles Muise, Jr.,
painted a raw pine desk for
me. He spent many long days
in residence working on the
piece, and my family began
to call Charles our itinerant
journeyman.*

Above: Charles Muise was inspired by decorative painting on old furniture. I gladly gave him carte blanche on this piece, with no regrets.

Left: In our bedroom, I've used a cheerful yet sophisticated floral design for the curtains and the duvet cover from Hinson & Co., which I never tire of coming home to.

Left: Dalto and Marine of Maine custom-designed a painted Shaker-style chest from my description of an old piece I'd once seen. The vintage fabric-covered boxes are a few of many stacked throughout the apartment. These were made by Ivy Weitzman.

Above: The green painted chest of twenty-seven tiny drawers was bought at five in the morning during the "early bird" hours of an antiques show. The chest, dating from the mid-1800s, was said to have been used in a factory, probably by a printer, because it could hold the letters of the alphabet plus punctuation marks in the extra drawer. The drawers were thoroughly coated with a fine metal soot. Cleaned up, they provide plenty of room now for my costume jewelry—if only I could remember which necklace is in which drawer!

Above left: The earliest quilt I own dates from 1840–50 and contains a profusion of mid-nineteenth-century fabrics, my favorites.

TOUCHES
OF
WHIMSY

HAT-AND-THE-HEART TOUCH

Ingrid Savage, co-owner of Seattle's Hat and the Heart, recalls that, even as a child, she had a passion for collecting. She counted agates, seed pods, wishing rocks, trolls from Sweden, and anything with hearts among her cherished possessions. A strong family tradition of collecting may have played a role in the way Savage has always surrounded herself with meaningful treasures. Her parents collected rare letters of nineteenth-century poets, ornately bound friendship books, and other Victorian ephemera, and their love for the small and unusual keepsake seems to have been passed along.

The house on Lake Washington is a welcoming 1921 Dutch colonial. A constant parade of children, friends, and neighbors enters through the kitchen, where they are greeted by the aroma of Walla Walla sweet onions stewing in a soup and a drain board filled with fresh-cut roses from the garden. Savage cooks and arranges flowers in the same unaffected and effortless way she deals with her decorative accessories. Her style of decorating is never a chore or a challenge; it provides pleasure and satisfaction.

Ingrid Savage is open to the spontaneous and the unexpected. When she and her business partner, Diane Glenn, were seeking a name for their shop, they came across a photograph of an old quilt square having two symbols appliquéd within: a black top hat and a red heart. The symbolism seemed so striking and so immediate that the shop

Left: The many coats and hats on the Victorian tortoised bamboo hat and umbrella stand tell something about the busy family that lives in this 1921 Dutch colonial house in Seattle. The leaded glass doors leading to the living room are common to Northwest houses of this period.

Left: A counterbalance with a lead-weighted star occupies a place on the mantel. The intricately carved frame, with its unusual doily design, is an example of early-twentieth-century tramp art. Shoes from Savage's collection, including Victorian, glass, and china shoes, sit on the mantel.

suddenly had a name: Hat and the Heart.

The very same spirit of spontaneity is evident throughout the interiors. Elaborate Victorian bird cages have been nonchalantly set on tabletops; a dining alcove is humorously crowded with old Halloween jack-o'-lanterns and chunky turkey candles that are forbidden to flame; international folk art blends in on shelves filled with family memorabilia and old books. Because she supports contemporary artists of the Northwest, Savage is proud to point out the work of such local painters as Cooper Edens, James Martin, Julie Paschkis, and Lynn Votaw. At their shop, she and Glenn hold shows for artisans whose work they wish others to know more about.

Whether she's buying for her shop or for herself, Ingrid Savage knows her main criterion will always be "Do I like to look at it?" She quickly rejects contrived or overly serious pieces that seem out of sync with her instinctive selection process. Quirky pieces with a history—a festooned sailor's valentine, an unusual screen mask, a fussy tramp-art frame—hold the greatest appeal. And objects with certain motifs—hearts, hands, and crows in particular—find places in her home just when every surface seems occupied. Without fanfare, Ingrid Savage has assembled the treasures of her family's life into a decorating scheme of enduring charm and personal expression.

Left and above: The living room contains furniture that once belonged to one of the owners's great-grandparents. Moon motifs on the chair fabric are the first of many such motifs found throughout the house. The bird cage is Victorian, but the bird held captive was made by the Washington wood-carver Michael Zitka. Moons were scavenged from local junk shops.

Above: Rooms flow one into the other in this generous and inviting family home.

Right: An old bird cage holds eggs colored by the children and their friends. The crow is by Michael Zitka.

Below left: There's a treasure trove of other majolica pieces stored in closets because display space, such as this break-front, has simply run out! The crystal chandelier makes a successful play of opposites against the Hitchcock chairs and French country table.

Above: Every room is filled with beloved collectibles and furniture with a history.

Top: Wild strawberries from the garden fill a favorite majolica pitcher.

Above: There's a shelf within a shelf here, a small green one of unknown age and origin that was bought for its charm alone. The grouping also includes a doll from Goodwill, a South American mask, Norwegian salt boxes, and a favorite children's book.

Above: The painted tin and glass cupboard is filled with a medley of Victorian ephemera and memorabilia, including a miniature shoe collection, pillboxes, and other unusual small collectibles that suit the owner's fancy.

Left: Savage doesn't need an occasion to bring out her mercury glass collection.

Left: The tone of the bedroom is soft and warm, enhanced further by the use of three vintage quilts. Both bed quilts, thought to be English, were remarkable junk shop finds. The Dresden Plate quilt on the wall was found at a Goodwill thrift shop. The Danish oak bed was found by the Savages on a trip to Denmark.

Below: The etching of a woman's hands is from Mexico. The Victorian frames hold family portraits.

Above: Generations of memories decorate the wall above the bamboo sewing table in the bedroom.

Above: Two tin ex-votos, meant to be hung in thanks for a miracle, are Greek.

Above: There are barely enough shelves and cupboards to hold everything.

Far right: Greek and Sicilian ex-votos of bodies and body parts seem to have an appropriate spot near the tub.

Above: Savage is "weathering" a brand-new windmill in her yard for Michael Zitka.

Left and right: The garden and yard overlook Lake Washington.

TOWN-HOUSE FANTASY

Visitors to this Victorian town house in New York City have the distinct feeling that Peaches Gilbert and the Mad Hatter would have gotten along famously. Peaches, whose real first name is used only for official occasions, was given her nickname by childhood friends because of her fair, "peachy" appearance, and the name has stuck. As if on cue, two rambunctious Wheaton terriers suddenly bound down the staircase, looking a bit like Tweedledee and Tweedledum. The fantasy has begun.

Most people think that Peaches Gilbert's first name is Mabel, because her thoroughly original Madison Avenue store is called Mabel's. But Mabel was actually Peaches's beloved cat, who did wind sprints through the house and sang in the middle of the night. Mabel best represented the image that Peaches wanted for her store—soft and elegant but whimsical. Mabel's image also best represents the many handcrafted decorative accessories adorned with animal themes, eagerly sought after by animal lovers, that Gilbert sells in her store.

Gilbert's passion for animals is apparent throughout her home, where a formal European atmosphere is regularly punctuated with whimsy and wit. Stuffed bears of every description are jammed into a glass-front cupboard, where they must constantly make room for yet another fuzzy chum. Porcelain peaches, picked up on travels, decorate mantels and tabletops. And there are cats to be found in every room—the late Mabel represented in every conceivable medium by the artists and artisans that Gilbert works with.

Gilbert believes that one's possessions are a

Left: The artisan Monte Lindsay designed this willow bed, which transforms the bedroom into a forest retreat.

Left: The bright papier-mâché birds by Jolean Albright have been given an amusing camouflage by the table skirt.

definite personal reflection of who the owner really is. She puts her personal stamp on a room not so much by the furniture, she says, but by the many accessories that make up her own "small biography." This biography results in a decorating scheme that combines folksy and formal, adds generous portions of wit, and never strains at matching or coordinating.

Gilbert is constantly changing and rearranging. She brings in new accessories from her store to try them out at home. A visit generally includes a tour with an interesting commentary about the origin and craft of the many pieces that threaten to leave no surface or wall space uncovered. This is not a concern for Gilbert, who always finds a place for things she loves—which are marvelous and many.

Above: The painter David Stein created a large landscape for Gilbert's intimate dining alcove. The contemporary Italian chairs are paired with an Art Moderne table. The chandelier is French.

Left: Vintage linens and Barbara Eigen's terra-cotta dinner pieces mix the past and the present with style.

Above: Mabel the painted wood cat is meant for shelf sitting. A piece on her back slips between two books and keeps Mabel on her perch.

Left: A hand-hooked backgammon rug gives the game an unusual twist.

Above: Gilbert's wonderfully eccentric collection of objects appears spontaneously arranged. What appears to be an old child's shoe is actually a wooden sculpture from France.

Left: The predictable is carefully avoided by Gilbert, who advocates the use of instinct and whimsy when it comes to decorative accessories. Here, a merry Saint Nicholas pillow is settled all-year-round among the more elegant designs.

Right: Gilbert's outrageous menagerie of bears in all sizes, shapes, and conditions began as a childhood passion and continues today.

Above: A lizard on a chair becomes expected in this town house of surprise touches. Mary Bowman of New Mexico created the lizard from felt. The lamp has been hand painted to resemble verdigris.

Left: Cats come in all sizes in the Gilbert household. This cat—a painting by Yoriko Iketani—appears tempted by Gilbert's fanciful roosters, collected over the years, which have outgrown their place of honor in the kitchen.

Above: Created as a wedding gift for Gilbert and her husband, the wall art is a tin work by Bruce Sprinkles.

Above right: An endearing assemblage of Gilbert's Madison Avenue storefront was a gift from her daughter.

Right: Brightly painted tin works by Magda Shumer hang in the Gilbert kitchen.

FOLK-ART INFLUENCE

HIGH STYLE WITH FOLK ART

The husband and wife owners of a gracious New York City apartment filled with period American antiques and an outstanding collection of folk art are among the rare few who fulfill an absolute definition of "collector." Their intelligent approach to collecting brings museum-quality furniture and unusual primitive pieces into their family's life-style.

Assisting with the development and promotion of the Museum of American Folk Art in New York has been an all-consuming interest of the owners for nearly a decade. Throughout the apartment, folk art coexists perfectly with highly polished period furniture and silver. Primitive objects such as a Conestoga wagon hitch or the expressive head of a nineteenth-century ventriloquist's dummy have been selected both for their history and their design.

These collectors attend auctions and also assist as volunteers for the Museum of American Folk Art. They will often recognize the originality of some piece that others had simply overlooked. It's this ability to discover the uniqueness of an object in a fashionable gallery or an open-air market that makes the difference. The result is a decorating scheme that offers a feast for the eye and a treat for the intellect.

As visitors pass from one room to the next, they soon feel blissfully removed from the busy city many floors below. The symmetry and balance of warm-

Left: Polished to perfection, the period furniture is a graceful complement to the early hooked rug and primitive eighteenth-century portrait by an unknown Connecticut artist. Formal pieces exist in perfect harmony with folk art old and new.

Left: A whimsical cat hooked rug, in mint condition even though it is nearly seventy years old, seems all-knowing, its place elevated from floor to wall. The tartan-design trinket box is from Maine. The horse is Staffordshire.

toned furniture with the many unique decorative objects leave one sensing that a pristine precision and delicate organization are at work. Objects are carefully arranged with a curator's devotion, then rearranged on a whim for variety. Graceful small table arrangements contribute to the feeling of elegance and serenity. Fresh-cut peonies from the country fill Chinese vases that overflow with natural beauty.

The owners say there is no great mystery to putting together a collection that is both livable and meant for generations to follow. It is simply a matter of learning a lot, looking at everything, and following your own good instincts when it comes to investing in what you wish to live with for a very long time.

Above: Contemporary folk art makes a decorative statement in this unexpected arrangement. The carved and painted giraffe was bought by one of the owners, a Museum of American Folk Art trustee, at the museum's shop. The Santa Fe painting was done in the 1940s by Doris Lee. The rest of the pieces and objects are from the past, making a successful mix of old and new.

Left: Dutch and English brass snuffboxes; fresh-cut peonies from the country.

Above: These collectors believe in mixing their treasures to create areas of special interest, such as this recessed clam shelving.

Above: Unusual polychrome decorated flasks share a place with Staffordshire figurines.

Far right: The head for a ventriloquist's dummy is given a pedestal and suitably treated as an objet d'art, sitting among fine Dutch and English antique objects.

Above: The airy Central Park view is a pretty setting for an unusual table arrangement. A Conestoga wagon wheel hitch becomes sculpture and is placed next to a 1980 work by the artist Susan Rothenberg.

Right: The colors are inviting, the furniture is comfortable, and the late afternoon sun warms and welcomes family and friends after a long day.

Above: A prominent horse weather vane, attributed to the J. Howard Co., circa 1850, is a focal point of the library. There's a vintage Bloomingdale's price sticker, now so worn that the price has faded from sight, on the back of the painted plate. The plate's pattern goes perfectly with the sofa's floral chintz.

QUIET COMPOSITIONS, UNDERSTATED TREASURES

O n a village street lined with trees that date back even further than the houses they shelter, it would be easy to pass a modest but charming old house that blends in with its natural surroundings. The appearance of this 1904 shingle-style cottage, owned by Jill Keefe and her husband, John Kois, belies the two generations of collections that are just inside the door.

This East Hampton, Long Island, house envelops its guests with warmth and low-keyed serenity. Keefe and her husband, a publishing consultant and former disc jockey who collects rare books and an outstanding variety of compact discs,

are attracted to uniform colors and a nineteenth-century palette. They find these colors more comforting, believing subtler colors allow the art and objects to be appreciated without distraction.

Jill Keefe says she inherited her love for fine art and folk art—old and new—from her mother, who was a decorator, collector, and world traveler. Trading art and objects within the family was something Keefe began doing at an early age. When she eventually inherited the contents of five houses filled with collectibles, Keefe made room for many of them in her own home and her life. She says that she now acquires only the things she loves. Because she started out with a solid collection, she says she can afford to be selective. The resulting arrange-

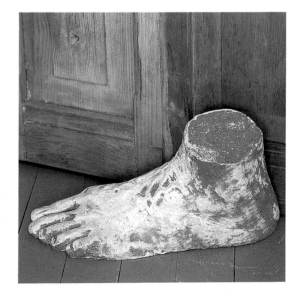

Left: An inviting small hallway holds everything one needs to venture out- doors. The handwoven tapestry rug is by Sara Hotchkiss.

Left: Keefe likes to think this plaster cast of a foot—a perfect door- stop—is the foot of a local artist, possibly de Kooning or Pollock.

ments reflect the care of a discriminating curator.

Keefe has a special fondness for primitive art and craft and an affinity for black-and-white dog figures. Sitting and lying about in various poses and sizes, these charming and unusual folk-art dogs become a constant theme running throughout the house. Two frisky real-life dogs, one black and white, seem to fit right in.

The many carved figures and vessels in the house are displayed with ease and without fanfare because they are such an integral part of the surroundings. Mexican pots, American jugs, and European crystal vases hold a colorful array of flowers from the garden.

There is no lack of display surface in the Keefe-Kois house, including two bronze coffee tables, painted chests, and several French antique carved wood tables. The mix of furniture is eclectic; the wood finishes are deep and frequently embellished with hand carving. Art and objects are displayed in pleasing compositions, then changed and interchanged frequently.

Jill Keefe thoroughly enjoys the details in her home, treating them not like possessions but trusted old friends.

Above: Fresh vegetables in a Papago Indian basket on Daniel Hale's whimsical tea table mimic the painting above.

Left: Green painted floors and white walls act as background for the deep tones of the furniture and the details, including Bill King's wall sculpture and an anonymous local artist's folk-art dog made from split-rail fence posts.

Above: The figures are African and Pre-Columbian; the jug is American; the lamp is by Giacometti; the collage is by Claudia Whitman and appears to have been made to go with just this arrangement.

Above: The colors in a lithograph by Man Ray echo those in the wooden ark by Daniel Hale, whose work is sought after in the Keefe-Kois home.

Far right: Baroque silver candlesticks from Ireland are at home with English chairs, a Biedermeier table, an original French chandelier, and a newly hooked rug.

Right: The original paint of the French trumeau, *or mirror with painting, sets the tone for a home that is filled with treasures valued for the age they show.*

Below: The mysterious face on one of a pair of old andirons brought back from Austria seems uncomfortable being watched so closely.

Above: The unusual garden trophy above the fireplace was made by an artist from Martinique for Keefe's uncle, who gave it to her when she was only five years old. The black-and-white wooden dog by an unknown early-twentieth-century artist—one of many figures of this theme—appears to guard the hearth.

Above: Textures and weaves speak for themselves in this bedroom close-up.

Left: Truly a one-of-a-kind piece, this dressing table mirror contains countless commemorative tokens from the First World War. The lamp, a cast of a Roman head, sheds light on an arrangement of personal objects.

Right: Keefe discovered a stock of old shutters during a trip to Mexico and planned her bedroom renovation around them. The deep earthen tone colors of the room are picked up by the reversible quilt, a handwoven rug, and pillows made from antique kilims.

RIDE ON A CAROUSEL

It seemed fitting that two gentle horses should be standing at the gate across the road from a converted barn owned by a woman who has filled her home with many details related to horses and riding.

When the property of an early-twentieth-century horse farm on eastern Long Island was being developed, the exceptional barn and other outbuildings were mercifully saved for remodeling. The barn was gutted and remodeled several years ago by a previous owner. The new owner, a Wall Street trader, was treated to an artistic and airy renovation. She named the residence "The Brass Ring," her country place for weekend tennis, swimming, and, of course, horseback riding.

The designer Susan Anthony was called in to work with the busy woman executive, who had strong tastes, a penchant for things country, and an attic filled with old family treasures. Not one purchase was made for the new house before an inventory was taken of every last antique, accessory, and piece of furniture in the attic. With that accomplished, finding places for old things and acquiring new things could begin.

Antique and flea markets from Maine to Maryland were scoured for the just-right touches. Susan Anthony came across an old prop business selling off all the things it had rented to clients over the years for movies and ads. There she discovered two exceptional carousel horses. They were mounted on their carousel bases in the great open stairwell of the house, where they appear to fly.

Since both the client and decorator liked working with bright colors and country pieces in a spare and sophisticated way, they had no trouble agreeing on a plan for every room. It is no wonder that the

Left: Shadow and Barbados graze in a paddock fenced off from the parking area, making visitors to The Brass Ring immediately aware that the house was once a home for horses.

Left: The antique carousel horse, prominently mounted on half its original swivel base, was found in a New York State store that sold props, mainly for advertising and film.

project came together in record time.

Knowing when to stop accessorizing and allow country things to take their places as art and not become lost among clutter is also a skill that client and decorator have in common. The combination of clean, lyrical space, tasteful design work, and touches that hold meaning makes this collaboration a prize-winning brass ring.

Below: Newly crafted, a graceful wooden swan is a perfect fit for this inviting nook, located a few steps beyond the stairway and secluded from the rest of the ground floor.

Below right: The British pine ladder in the background is a novel approach to display.

Above: Visitors may hang their coats and hats on this brass coat rack in a weekend home where horse and riding themes abound.

Left: The rather formal etchings once belonged to the owner's grandmother and were found in the family's attic when the decoration of the house was under way. Other treasures from the attic include a nineteenth-century quilt and an old watering can, said to be from a farm near Paris.

Right: Reproduction pine chairs around the dining table have been given painted accents. The chandelier is cut tin, newly made, and was bought on the West Coast. An old tool box provides a display container for the flowering begonias.

Below: Certainly this British plate rack must have come from a grand estate. Here, it becomes a perfect room divider as well.

Below left: The spare and symmetrical arrangement on the painted cupboard creates formality from informal country pieces.

Above: Since the entire ground floor of the renovated barn, once horse stalls, is now an open space, it is necessary that furniture and accessories define the various living areas. Bright floral chintz sofas create an intimate seating arrangement by the fireplace. The generous dried wreath by Gail Peachin is the perfect year-round flower arrangement.

Left: Sunlight streams through pine shutters into a bedroom that brings together some of the owner's favorite possessions—the bright quilt, the braided rug, and the wallpapered bandboxes in the primitive cupboard.

Above: There's a brief family history in this one small corner of the guest bedroom. The old school desk belonged to the owner's mother (the framed photographs are of her and her brother); the books are family attic finds.

Above: A rooster weather vane from Vermont can find a home in just about any setting, and has surely found one here.

Above: Another year-round wreath adorns a door. Because the owner uses her home on weekends and holidays only, she enjoys the carefree beauty that dried everlastings offer.

Left: It seems appropriate that the owner, a tennis enthusiast, should have found an old tennis bench for her porch. The windmill is American and is set out every weekend.

Right: It is hoped that passing geese are tempted by these decoys to land. The wooden figures are from Prince Edward Island and date back to the 1920s. The large guards protect the smaller feeders, as in nature.

Above: Each piece of dinnerware by the Texas ceramicist Claudia Reese is one of a kind. In keeping with the uniqueness of the dinnerware, cotton napkins in stripes and plaids are used, and each napkin is different.

COTTAGE STYLE

CREATIVE LABORS

The height and breadth of a full-blooming hydrangea tree in the yard, nestled close to the bungalow-style cottage, offers visitors a clue to the age of Diane Fisher's early-twentieth-century house by the Atlantic shore. Fisher, who once worked in the garment industry, claims that earnings from polyester pull-ons enabled her to buy the house twelve years ago. Since that time, renovating and decorating it with little outside advice or assistance has become an all-consuming avocation.

Fisher's city apartment and country home are worlds apart. In the city she lives contentedly with black lacquer, gray flannel, and Biedermeier. She knew she wanted a warm, unpretentious home away from home—something country but "not too cluttered and not *too* country." Fortunately, Fisher's mother, an antiques collector, had furniture and a few decorative accessories to spare, which helped out with the initial decorating. Then Fisher rented a van and drove through the Pennsylvania countryside in search of beds, rugs, quilts, vintage table linens, and anything else that would fit in.

Hunting in the country became a necessity. "I had the taste but not the money for New York City prices," she said. Little by little, country roads led Fisher to shops and flea markets off the beaten path and gave her the choices she needed to put her look together.

Fisher's creative labors on her cottage actually led her into a rewarding new career. In 1982, Lee Bailey, the designer and author of many successful food, gardening, and entertaining books, literally knocked on her front door to inquire if he might photograph her wicker-filled porch for a new book.

Left: A tall hydrangea tree in the backyard provides unlimited fresh-cut bouquets, which are then dried for the winter months.

Left: Vintage wicker on the front porch of this charming cottage evokes a gracious scene from times past.

After admiring the way Fisher had selected and arranged the eclectic mix of antiques and objects throughout the house, Bailey suggested she might consider creating her own line of accessories. Without further coaxing, Fisher put together what she describes as "a weird combination of little things—potholders, place mats, aprons, and napkins." She sent her wares to several shops and department stores and received an enthusiastic response to one item—a fresh and cheerful napkin. Suddenly, Fisher says, she had a business based on one napkin! Now, the napkin selection from Tablescenes is among the industry's finest.

Work on the cottage continues to provide weekend pleasure. The garden has grown from a small plot off the back porch into an elaborate rose garden that extends behind a garage-turned-guesthouse. Closets are jammed full of appealing linens from Fisher's business—mostly extras and seconds, she says. Fisher, a veteran magazine clipper, continues to glean ideas from others, and she continues to arrange and rearrange her country house, which is not too cluttered and not too country, but inimitably her own.

Above: In keeping with her easy style of table setting, Fisher uses an array of candleholders and related objects on an exquisite cut-work tablecloth. Here, Daniel Mack's rustic dowel candle-holders sit alongside a bobbin fitted for a candle and a white stoneware candle encircled by a Dianna Isola wreath. The terra-cotta din-nerware is by Barbara Eigen.

Left: The 1920s cottage has modest, well-proportioned rooms and an abundance of light.

Left: Fisher feels that the universal geometric designs and earth-tone colors of Indian baskets, blankets, and pottery allow them to be used in a variety of settings, either as accents or in major groupings.

Above and left: This quiet corner contains cherished collectibles and found objects, including a child's bowling set, a small bundle of driftwood, a pitcher of dahlias, a basket of pine cones, and a hand-painted box by two women artisans from Maryland who call themselves The Friends. The gnarled branches were gathered from the nearby ocean beach.

Right: When it comes to the sunny breakfast room, Fisher finds herself mixing and matching anything blue. The blue agateware was part of her mother's collection. Odd pieces of blue spongeware and antique blueware are always welcome additions to the china cupboard, without regard to their patterns. Blue-and-white tablecloths are layered for a soft, graceful effect. Fisher enjoys buying country chairs, each one different from the next. It's her relaxed and confident "anything goes" attitude that creates a room with personal expression.

Above: Cosmos and ageratum make a pretty picture.

Above: The nostalgic "Lemon Meringue Pie" sign reminded Fisher of an era when the kitchen was the busiest and warmest room in the house. The sign was found in a local thrift shop. The humorous 1920s juicers belonged to her mother.

Right: The apple cookie jars and condiment containers are from the 1920s, the same vintage as the house they occupy.

Above: Over the past several years, Diane Fisher has custom-ordered favorite pieces from The Valkris Pottery. She is especially attached to the blue designs, with their graceful shapes and their many uses.

ARTISTIC ARRANGEMENTS

When Linda Cheverton and her husband, photographer Walter Wick, brought an overflow of furniture and decorative accessories from their city apartment to their newly acquired country home, they took a novel approach to decorating. For Cheverton, a photo stylist (someone who shops for and arranges the props, objects, and flowers for editorial and advertising pages of magazines and newspapers), decorating meant seeing the possibility for countless pleasing arrangements for their own belongings. Cheverton feels that most people take one look at empty rooms and fill them first with larger pieces, saving the finishing touches for last. Her way is quite the opposite. The result is a profusion of delightful vignettes through-

out their nineteenth-century house that make it picture perfect.

Cheverton is a professional shopper. She spends her days searching for unusual objects that will put her signature on the styling she has developed. Her Connecticut home, a weekend retreat, frequently becomes a testing ground for recent acquisitions. Inevitably, most of what is in her home ends up in a photograph, and vice versa. She relies on many of her personal possessions to put together the week's assignments. Too often, she says, she develops a strong attachment to an object used for a shot and ends up buying it for herself.

A chest in the dining room is filled with vintage linens—a damask tablecloth with the deep crease marks of many years, a set of embroidered napkins from the 1920s, and an intricate cut-work luncheon set in need of cleaning and repair, but otherwise

Left: The furniture maker Daniel Mack says his bench in Cheverton's entranceway is styled after a medieval tuffet, used for courting. Legend has it that the bench's planterlike areas were meant to be filled with sweet-smelling herbs to surround the young lovers with pleasant fragrances.

Left: The miniature Windsor chairs by Gerald Headley of Virginia are signed and dated. The oil painting is from 1840, artist unknown. The dog object is actually an old shooting gallery target from about 1880 that Cheverton and Wick decided to mount on a stand for the mantel.

perfect. The crisp pile of linens, all flea-market finds, were generally bought early in the morning as dealers unpacked their wares. As "tablescaper" for *Food and Wine* magazine covers, Cheverton has a trained eye when it comes to spotting special old things that make the difference between just accessorizing and accessorizing with panache. "If you see something that's unique, don't pass it up." Cheverton takes her own advice, and it shows.

Although the house dates from the late nineteenth century, Cheverton and Wick do not stick to a period style of decorating. Their interest in modern photography, contemporary pottery, and decorative objects from the Southwest works together with their taste for both primitive and refined country things. As a stylist, Cheverton has resisted a monotony of style by trying daring combinations.

With the admirable ease and a cheerful enthusiasm for what Cheverton and Wick clearly like to do, it becomes evident that instinct and risk taking are elements of this decorating success story.

Above: It pleases Cheverton to establish a mood and a unique setting with the things she loves. Here, a vase of fresh flowers sits out of harm's way atop a fine tin pie safe.

Left: The nineteenth-century crib quilt is a prized possession of the owners, as is the Joe Ortega rabbit.

Left: In the dining room, elegant and uncluttered, the country pieces may be dressed up or down, depending on the occasion. The chandelier, a 1930s reproduction of a nineteenth-century fixture, has been electrified so that it may be used with or without candles. The Scandinavian pine chairs are appealing for their simplicity and clean design. As a fanciful touch, Cheverton has draped one window with a valance of cattails.

Above: Cheverton, a believer in the art of the unmatched, displays her Roseville, Van Briggle, and Rookwood Art Pottery along with contemporary pieces in this delightful asymmetrical sideboard arrangement.

Above: Rough-hewn and rustic, the dough bin provides an interesting surface for Paul Perras's limestone sculpture entitled Hammer-headed Num.

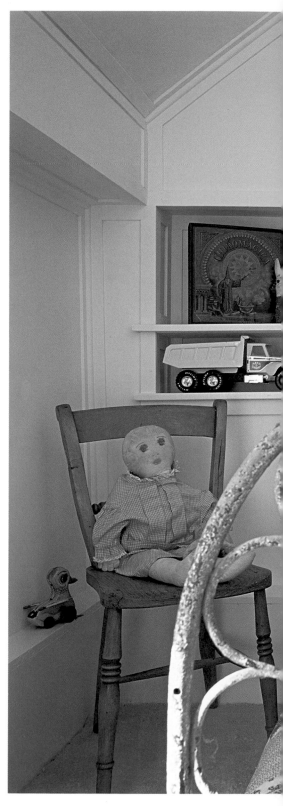

Above: A primitive head made from a wood shingle keeps company with bowls by the contemporary potter Adele Broitman.

Left: Cheverton liked what the years had done to the original finish of this child's iron bed and decided against cleaning it up with restoration. Walter Wick's vintage game collection is displayed on the shelves. His educational poster for children adds punch and color to this small room meant for small guests.

Right: A colorful splash of Fiestaware, set on a shaded screened-in porch off the living room, with vintage white linens, has personal flair. Cheverton is constantly on the lookout for Fiestaware at local flea markets, where the prices are better but rising all the same.

Above: Cheverton planned the comb-painted porch floor. Wick gave it an artist's touch.

HOMAGE TO PURE COUNTRY

A converted carriage house just forty-five minutes from midtown Manhattan became the perfect home for a young couple who wanted to bring their sophisticated yet relaxed decorating ideas to a traditional setting in the country. An architect and director of Marshall Cummings in New York, Lawrence Mufson says that he and his wife, Ralph Lauren clothing designer Melanie Bendavid, rely mainly on instinct when it comes to furnishing and decorating their new home. "There is never a plan. We just let things grow free-form," he said.

So, two years ago, Mufson and Bendavid simply gave the rooms a fresh coat of white paint and moved in. At this point they were ready to head for auctions, tag sales, antiques shops, and local barn sales to fill the empty spaces.

But at first Mufson resisted country decorating. His classical training as an architect made him wary that his home might turn into all the things he was taught to eschew, becoming cluttered and "too cute." He soon realized that many straightforward principles of design—honesty, integrity, and durability—could be found in American folk and primitive pieces. Furthermore, he loved the whimsy and frequent silliness of certain folk objects, which become bold statements for art and design when they are displayed in uncrowded spaces. Mufson soon became a convert.

Left: Late one night, when driving past an antiques shop, Mufson and Bendavid spotted a grand-scale bird cage displayed in a brightly lit window. The next day they returned to buy it. The cage, made by a father for his children, now stands behind a handsome tapestry sofa.

Left: A small mantel holds a bird's nest from the yard and an unusual collection of marble eggs from Italy. Fragrant dried flowers are from the "drying factory" in the attic. An old bird-house and an early jug from Mufson's collection of stoneware complete the picture.

Melanie Bendavid was influenced by her work with Ralph Lauren, whose clothing collections are designed in relation to their surroundings. The charming and innocent mood she creates as part of her job translates into the way she sees her own home. She says that "creating historical illusion comes naturally."

Arrangements of everlastings fill the air with the sweetness of outdoors. The attic has been made into what Mufson and Bendavid humorously refer to as their "drying factory." There they have set up racks for garden flowers grown especially for everlastings. This common interest provides a never-ending supply for their home and original gifts for family and friends.

Mufson and Bendavid try to maintain a certain simplicity. They pull back when the interiors feel crowded or cluttered. As a couple, they feel that their home is never finished, always evolving. The pleasure for them is in the means, not in the end.

Above: The corner cupboard added by former owners in 1930 means space to display family things, including Mufson's mother's Tiffany silver and nineteenth-century British china.

Left: Mufson spotted the antique table turned upside down in a barn sale. Dusted off and polished, it is a sweet match for the Pennsylvania balloon-back chairs. Floral fabrics both new and old cover pillows on the inviting window seat.

Left: The traditional Irish furniture and accessories in the dining room are used in a clean, spare way, a reflection of Mufson's architectural background. The chandelier is a faithful reproduction by a Connecticut artisan.

Below left and right: The still life, a Currier and Ives print, imitates the fresh-picked apples and pears in a hand-carved bowl on the early blanket chest.

Above: Miniature gourds, dried corn, and berries are combined in a natural autumn arrangement.

153

Above: Bendavid collects 1930s "French ivory" pieces because she is drawn to the color. The sweet American sampler is done in cross-stitch.

WESTERN
AESTHETICS

SUNSHINE AND SHADOWS

Geography has influenced Susan Parrish's choices more than any other element she can think of. Her obvious southwestern connection has its roots in her early years in Texas. Both her personal and professional life provide memories from the past. The muted Indian rug in her living room is the same rug she used on her college dorm-room floor.

When Parrish moved her antiques business from California to a shop in New York several years ago, the long cross-country drive through windswept desert areas strengthened her decision to retain a western style in a city given to more elaborate and trend-setting decorating. Dealing in Indian antiques and textiles, fine American quilts, and primitive furniture, Parrish would hold onto her treasured Navaho rugs and New Mexican pots and use them in her new home in a spare, sophisticated way. And she was determined to find a place for her cherished fiberglass cactus, a Hollywood set prop used in 1950s Westerns—a true conversation piece.

Parrish's converted loft is located in a former 1920s pharmaceuticals factory in a landmark section of Greenwich Village, New York City. The broad expanse of high windows with a Mary Poppins view casts constant daylight and evening shadows onto the interior space. Visitors are immediately awed by the beauty of the quilts on the bed and on the walls. Parrish, a quilt expert and exhibitor at the prestigious Fall Antiques Show in New York, bought over a hundred quilts in 1979—all at one time—thus fortifying her growing quilt business. At home and at her shop, Parrish says she does not

Left: The 1840s painted bench from New England was originally bought for Parrish's business; it now graces her entrance hall. The 1930s painting shows a penniless artist and his landlord. The 1920s Navaho rugs add color.

Left: Colorful Beacon blankets, found mainly in the West and Southwest, have gained sudden popularity with collectors. Parrish sells Beacon blankets at her Greenwich Village shop and enjoys having a few at home.

159

decorate, but rather puts things together, adding and subtracting as her tastes change.

There seems to be a quilt for every season, and Parrish's bedroom has become a veritable calendar. A quilt in soft summer colors is exchanged for one with autumnal tones at the first hint of fall; begonias are replaced with chrysanthemums. The westerner come east has found a way to celebrate seasonal changes while retaining a style that keeps her close to her roots.

Left and right: A small bed-room area is tucked into a light alcove. A green painted cupboard, with its original paint dating back to 1850, makes a roomy closet. The fiberglass cactus was used as a movie-set prop. The 1920s split-reed chair has its factory sticker, which reads: "Karpen Hand-Fiber."

Above: Most visitors must be told that this mysterious architectural detail is part of an ornate lightning rod. The small painting seems perfectly suited to the setting.

Right: Originally a 1920s Greenwich Village pharmaceuticals factory, the building was recently converted into imaginatively designed lofts with several platform levels. The primitive furniture and outstanding nineteenth-century Lone Star quilt help create a relaxed yet well-composed area for dining.

Above: The inspired design of the interior allows museum-quality pots from New Mexico a dramatic gallerylike presentation.

*Above: Parrish is a quick-
change artist when it comes to
her bed-making. Here, an
1860s chintz pieced quilt with
a glazed border is used with
pretty vintage linens. The art
on the wall is actually a pic-
torial beaded Navaho bag. A
crocheted spread has become
a delicate curtain.*

Above: Festive for the Fourth of July and any other time of the year, this crisp red, white, and blue color scheme is always a favorite.

Left: The somber Texas quilt made by German immigrants from suiting fabrics was meant for winter warmth.

165

Left: The early-twentieth-century split-reed chair has its original finish. The Roseville pot dates from the 1930s. David Swing's oil painting Deer Valley, Arizona *was done in 1925 and still has its original frame.*

Below: Parrish collects colorful old socks, which she loves to wear and, consequently, ends up mending frequently. The lady who watches is thought to be a 1930s counter display piece, signed "Esther Hunt." A lamp from the Arts and Crafts period mixes easily with Parrish's favorite armchair, which was recently upholstered in a bargello-inspired fabric. In the background on the windowsill, a collection of antique leather balls now serves as thoroughly original bookends.

Above: The Santa Fe potter Anthony Bowman created fantastic creatures to adorn his terra-cotta vase, which sits on a Japanese tansu chest. The 1870 quilt's design is known as Straight Furrows. Parrish keeps her jewelry in the English grained-wood box.

TAMING THE WILD WEST

Aspen Highlands, a Colorado mountain not recommended to the faint-hearted skier, ends in a graceful slope and is bordered by the trees it was named for. Judith and Bill Carr built their barn-red New England–style house within walking distance of this majestic slope, where they ski in the winter and hike when the snow has melted. For nearly a year, they lived in a run-down bungalow on the site and built a spacious and contemporary house literally around it, working daily with a construction crew that grew accustomed to spontaneous requests for a window here or a glass panel there to take advantage of the western light and magnificent views.

The interior of the house that the Carrs built is open and airy, designed with their many unusual antiques and folk art pieces in mind. Believing that it's not what you put in but what you leave out, they had assembled lively and frequently offbeat pieces and now wanted to enjoy them as part of an accessible decorating scheme. By painting the walls and woodwork white and upholstering furniture in the same fresh way, a stark and cool yet comfortable setting was ready to receive both their brightly colored folk art and their warm-toned Indian objects.

Avoiding what they refer to as "the confusion of color," the Carrs chose natural colors and textures for a setting that allows changing seasons to become a part of the interior design. The Carrs are content with the "nature" of things, both inside and out. The only patterns are those intrinsic to the weave of a Navaho rug, an Indian creel, or a Beacon blanket.

Bill Carr, an investment banker, has collected

Left: An affection for traditional New England exteriors is apparent at the front door of the Carr home.

Left: Colorado mementoes fill but never crowd the Carr house. The old wooden firkins were chosen for their deep, rich colors.

American folk art since he was a boy growing up in the Midwest. An avid duck hunter, he used to trade veteran hunters their heavy wooden decoys for light-weight plastic ones. Eventually, he amassed one of the finest decoy collections in the country.

Judith Carr worked as a photo stylist in Aspen and feels that this experience helped her develop an eye for the balance, composition, and design that make a room work. Her design preference is for primitive antiques played against a gallerylike background, made all the more exciting by the resulting contradictions. Her own style blossomed, eventually motivating her to work with interior-design clients. After seeing Carr's innovative style at work at home, a style distinctly American and primarily western, many clients could not resist asking for something just like it.

The Carrs will travel great distances as part of "the hunt" for interesting pieces. Going from Sotheby's in New York to the Indian Market in Santa Fe, they state frankly, "We never pass up an opportunity." Their ultimate hunt is for "things with a sense of humor, things that make us smile, things that gave someone else a lot of joy, and now that joy is coming our way."

Above: The Carrs believe that the textures and colors of the objects they collect are best seen against clean white walls.

Left: The Carrs spent more on the crating and shipping from Illinois to Colorado of this dandy 1930s soapbox racer than they did on the car itself! The extraordinary collection of wooden fish on the wall was found in the ramshackle cabin of Phillip Sirois, a Maine hermit. After Sirois's death, Bill Carr acquired a third of the total collection, which fills one wall of the living room.

Left: Sunlight and breathtaking mountain views dictate much of the house's architectural design. White upholstered pieces reflect the owners' need for a spare, airy background to display their Indian and folk-art treasures. Wonderful, well-traveled leather suitcases from the days of steamer cruises and elegant railway journeys have been stacked to make a clever coffee table for the safflowers.

Below: Hoping to avoid a conventional display of objects, the Carrs show off their early-twentieth-century fishing bobbins under glass. The hardy yellow wildflowers make a pretty arrangement in Aspenwood baskets.

Above: The characteristic knots and twists of the late-nineteenth-century Adirondacks rhododendron-root furniture create a natural artistry in design. This type of Adirondacks furniture is a rare find and, according to the Carrs, it is worth waiting years to locate pieces of this quality. A portion of Phillip Sirois's fish decoy collection can be seen on the wall beyond.

173

Right: The Carrs developed a passion for the decorative woods and painted finishes of Indian clubs—used in turn-of-the-century gymnasiums as standard muscle-building equipment, a sort of forerunner of free weights thought to have been mass-produced in India. Here, the growing collection is treated as sculpture on display.

Above: Books form a pedestal for the wooden crow, once an advertisement for Red Raven Splits liquor.

Above: Native Colorado lodge-pole pine has been used for the handcrafted bed by Miguel Velez.

Left: The vintage quilt is a thrifty mix of wool suiting samples, made at a time when nothing was wasted.

Right: A row of antique fishing creels adds to the western look of the bedroom.

176

Above and right: Inspired by thoughts of freedom and romance, a prisoner at Colorado State Prison in Canon City made this desk in the 1940s for his true love on the outside. The chair is an original, made of steer hide and horn. Designs have been burned into the wood and carved in relief in what appears to be a 1950s television interpretation of the West.

Above: Much of Judith Carr's Navaho turquoise-and-silver jewelry collection still contains the original trading company pawn tags, which are very small. These tags have such meaning for Carr that she would not think of removing them, even for a night out.

179

Left: Collections are carried into the kitchen and used as decoration to keep the cook happy.

Below: Hobby and art join together in the kitchen's outstanding arrowhead collection, assembled by one man over the course of a lifetime with a sense of design that sets it apart. Found in a western shop, the framed arrowheads came from an estate in Maryland.

Below right: There's a serene William Bailey quality to the still-life arrangement of Red Wing pottery in a corner of the kitchen.

Above: The dappled hobby horse sits on a landing leading to the kitchen.

181

Above: The backyard view is of the Aspen Highlands.

Right: The Sun Room, designed as a passive solar area, is a warm and welcoming spot for informal entertaining. Judith Carr likes to use outdoor furniture indoors, as she's done here with French garden chairs.

Above: The lighthearted appearance of this crow confirms that he was once a child's pull-toy.

RESOURCES

RESOURCES

Inspired by the wonderfully diverse styles in Formal Country, *we have tried to provide the names of a wide variety of antiques shops, craft galleries, and shops offering a variety of decorative furnishings. Many of these sources are personal favorites, and others come highly recommended. However, the list is not all inclusive; it is only a springboard for you as you discover sources of your own. We advise that you call ahead for hours.*

Canada

ALBERTA

Canada House
201 Bear St.
Banff, Alberta
1 (800) 419-1298
Specializing in Inuit, Native and wildlife stone sculpture, wildlife and western bronze, and original woodcarvings.

BRITISH COLUMBIA

Country Roots Furniture
247 E. First St.
North Vancouver, B.C. V7L 1B4
Specializing in Shaker, Amish, Mission and Harvest style furniture.

Quilts Etc.
3111 Thunderbird Cr
Burnaby, B.C., V5A 3G1
(604) 421-5520
1 (800) 503-8818
Featuring down pillows and duvets, beds, bed linens, bath accessories, and window coverings.

ONTARIO

Harvest House Furniture
1 Proctor Rd, Box 269
Schomberg, Ont. L0G 1T0
(905) 939-8606
and
3554 Yonge St., Box 2104, Stn. B
Richmond Hill, Ont. L4E 1A3
*Specializing in made-to-order bedroom,
diningroom, and home office furniture
crafted from pine, oak, cherry, and
quarter sawn oak.*

River Road Traditions
RR#3
Port Elgin, Ont., N0H 2C7
1(800) 263-8938
*A unique collection of period lighting,
tinware, and pine furniture.*

QUEBEC

Vanessa Benitz Imports
4913 Boulevard de Maison Neuve
Montreal
*House-style paint finish kits and
paintability stencils.*

Heidi's Country Gift Shop
538 Main Rd.
Hudson
(514) 458-5766
*Specializing in windchimes, lace, teddy
bears, pewter, and handcrafted gifts.*

United States

ALABAMA

Artisans: Matt Lippa or Elizabeth Schaaf
P.O. Box 256
Mentone, AL 35984
(256) 634-4037
*Mail order company dealing in antiques,
folk art and outsider art. Pieces range
from formal to eccentric.*

ARKANSAS

Pump & Circumstance
28 Spring Street
Eureka Springs, AK 72632
(501) 253-6644
*Furniture and decorative objects with a
rustic motif.*

CALIFORNIA

Adirondack Designs
350 Cypress St.
Fort Bragg, CA 95437
(800) 222-0343
Adirondack furniture, arbors, redwood benches.

Country Affaire/Elden Collection
1170 North Main
Orange, CA 92667
(714) 771-5999
Wood/iron combinations with coordinating colors. Wholesale.

East Meets West Antiques
658 North Larchmont Blvd.
Hollywood, CA 90004
(213) 461-1389
Antiques, accessories, quilts, textiles, country furnishings. Wholesale/retail.

Echo Home and Garden
3775 24th St.
San Francisco, CA 94114
(888) 282-3330
Elegant and simple bath, garden and home accessories.

Fillamento
2185 Fillmore St.
San Francisco, CA 94115
(415) 931-2224
Select range of home accessories with a perfect blend of country and city.

Firelight Glass
1000 42nd St.
Emeryville, CA 94608-3621
(501) 428-0607
Handblown glass oil candles. Wholesale/retail.

Heart's Ease
4101 Burton Dr.
Cambria, CA
(805) 927-5224
Baskets, wreaths, garlands, bouquets, herbs and spices, garden accessories.

Hollyhock
214 N. Larchmont Blvd.
Los Angeles, CA 90004
(323) 931-3400
Home fashion shop offering accessories and furniture, including their own down upholstery group.

Indigo Seas
123 North Robertson Blvd.
Los Angeles, CA 90048
(213) 550-8758
Antiques; interior design service.

Sue Fisher King
3067 Sacramento St.
San Francisco, CA 94115
(415) 922-7276
Specializing in linens, pottery, and decorative home furnishings.

Milagros Gallery
414 First Street E
Sonoma, CA 95476
(707) 939-0834
Specializing in hand-picked pottery crafted in small villages throughout Mexico.

Palecek
P.O. Box 225
Richmond, CA 94808-0225
(800) 274-7730
Wicker chairs, love seats and accessories.
Wholesale.

The Pine Mine
7974 Melrose Ave.
Los Angeles, CA 90046
(323) 653-9726
Specializing in English, French, Irish
and Welsh pine country furniture.

Pottery Barn
P.O. Box 7044
San Francisco, CA 94120-7044
(800) 588-6250
Kitchen and glassware, candlesticks,
pillows, bed and table linens, and
accessories for the home. Nationwide
locations. Catalog.

RH
2506 Sacramento Street
San Francisco, CA 94115
(415) 346-1460
A selection of pottery and garden objects.

Shabby Chic Furniture
1013 Montana Ave.
Santa Monica, CA 90404
(310) 394-1975
Oversized furniture with machine-
washable slipcovers.

The Snow Goose
1010 Torrey Pines Rd.
La Jolla, CA 92037
(619) 454-4893
American country furniture and folk art.

Wildgoose Chase
1936 South Coast Highway
Laguna Beach, CA 92651
(714) 376-9388
Antique Americana including quilts,
beacon blankets, pre-1900 antiques,
and painted furniture.

Terra Cotta
11925 Montana
Los Angeles, CA 90049
(323) 826-787
Formal furniture as well as country
pieces, lamps, mirrors, pillows and
related accessories.

COLORADO

The Artisan Center, Ltd.
2757 E. Third Ave.
Denver, CO 80206
(303) 333-1201
Pottery, textiles, and other crafts by
more than nine hundred American
contemporary artists.

Southwestern by Kopriva's
2445 E. Third Ave.
Denver, CO 80206
(303) 333-2299
Southwestern designs, including furniture,
lamps, custom pillows, rugs and
whimsical pieces.

CONNECTICUT

Country Folk
P.O. Box 211
Rowayton, CT 06853
(203) 655-6887
*Antique quilts, new folk art, china and
gift items*

James Dew & Son
1171 Boston Post Road
Guilford, CT 06437
(203) 453-3847
*Fine handcrafted reproduction American
furniture.*

EGH Peter, Inc.
Box 52
Norfolk, CT 06058
(203) 542-5221
*American 18th-and-19th-century painted
furniture, with an emphasis on original
finishes. By appointment only.*

Ethan Allen, Inc.
Ethan Allen Dr.
P.O. Box 1966
Danbury, CT 06813-1966
(203) 743-8000
*Upholstered chairs, sofas, and other fine
home furnishings. Wholesale.*

Main Street Cellar Antiques
120 Main St.
New Canaan, CT 06840
(203) 966-8348
*Country and high country furniture,
quilts, folk art, and Americana.*

Monique Shay Antiques
920 Main St. S
Woodbury, CT 06798
(203) 263-3186
*French and Canadian country antiques,
painted and natural pine furniture.*

Winsor Antiques
53 Sherman St.
Fairfield, CT 06430
(203) 255-0056

WASHINGTON D.C.

Appalachian Spring
1415 Wisconsin Ave. NW
Washington, D.C. 20007
(202) 337-5780
Contemporary American Crafts.

Park Place
2251 Wisconsin Ave. NW
Washington, D.C. 20007
(202) 342-6294
*Garden furnishings including Victorian-
style cast-aluminum chairs, teak
benches, and stone animals.*

Susquehanna Antique Co.
3216 O. St. NW
Washington D.C. 20007
(202) 333-1511
*Eighteenth-and nineteenth-century
furniture, painted pieces, quilts and
hooked rugs.*

FLORIDA

General Store
7920 NW 76th Ave.
Medley, FL 33164
(404) 577-8270
Country design furnishings. Wholesale.

When Pigs Fly
411 N. Donnelly St., #101
Mount Dora, FL 32757
1 (800) 974-4735
Primitives, folk art and traditional crafts.

GEORGIA

The Gables Antiques
711 Miami Circle NE
Atlanta, GA 30324
(404) 231-0734
*French country and English antiques,
    including porcelain objects.*

Simply Southern Furniture
P.O. Box 370
Industrial Blvd.
Toccoa, GA 30577
(706) 886-7454
Country-designed beds. Wholesale.

IDAHO

Ann Reed Gallery
620 Sun Valley Rd.
Ketchum, ID 83340
(208) 726-3036
*Fine art, furniture, Southwestern folk
    art, rustic furniture and fine crafts.*

ILLINOIS

Amish Folk Quilt Co.
10593 W. Touhy
Rosemont, IL 60018
(847) 827-5448
*Wooden crafts, quilts and wall hangings
    handcrafted by Amish women.*

Carl Hammer Gallery
200 W. Superior St.
Chicago, IL 60610
(312) 266-8512
American folk art and paintings.

David Kay
One Jenni Lane
Peoria, IL 61614-3198
(800) 535-9917
*Garden accessories, furniture, wall
    decorations. Catalog.*

INDIANA

Acorn Family Antiques
15466 Oak Rd.
Carmel, IN 46032
(317) 846-6257
*Formal and country antique American
    furniture, paintings, silver, and
    fine china.*

Basketry and Crafts by Karen
405 Laurel Lane
Madison, IN 47250
(812) 265-6164

Country Gardener
491 West State Rd., 114
North Manchester, IN 46962
(219) 982-4707
*Unique birdhouses, garden ornaments,
    herbs, everlastings. Wholesale/retail.*

Thomas H. Kramer, Inc.
805 Depot St., Commerce Pk
Columbus, IN 47201
(812) 379-4097
*Regional custom builders of country
    furniture.*

Parrett/Lich Inc.
2164 Canal Lane
Georgetown, IN 47122
(812) 951-3454
*American country furniture, folk art,
    and quilts.*

Tell City Chair Company
P.O. Box 369
Tell City, IN 47586
(812) 547-3491
*Solid wood chairs in various styles and
    sizes. Wholesale.*

KANSAS

American Star Buck
P.O. Box 15376
Lenexa, KS 66215
(913) 894-1567
*Pencil-post reproductions in pine, oak,
    maple, cherry, mahogany, ash, and
    walnut.*

KENTUCKY

Boone's Antiques of Kentucky, Inc.
4996 Old Versailles Rd.
Lexington, KY 40510
(606) 254-5335
*Antique English and French country
    and formal furniture and accessories.*

Cabin Creek Farm
Hannah and Art Stearns
P.O. Box 22
Mount Sherman, KY 42764
(502) 932-6227
Large selection of baskets, mostly antiques.

MAINE

Abacus Gallery
44 Exchange St.
Portland, ME 04101
(207) 772-4880
Contemporary and traditional crafts.

Handworks Gallery
Main Street
Blue Hill, ME 04614
Open summer, fall, and Christmas
Traditional and contemporary crafts.

R. Jorgensen Antiques
502 Post Rd.
Wells, ME 04090
(207) 646-9444
Country and formal period antiques.

Maine Cottage Furniture
P.O. Box 935
Lower Falls Landing
Yarmouth, ME 04096
(207) 846-1430
Cottage-inspired furniture and accessories.

Kenneth and Ida Manko
Box 20
Moody, ME 04054
(207) 646-2595
American folk art.

Schueler Antiques
10 High St. (Route 1)
Camden, ME 04843
(207) 236-2770
*American period furniture, paintings,
    accessories, primitives, folk art, and
    rare decoys.*

MARYLAND

Stella Rubin Antiques
12300 Glen Rd.
Potomac, MD 20854
(301) 948-4187
*Antique quilts, hooked rugs, and
    decorative accessories.*

Village House
103 Cross Street
Chestertown, MD 33162
(410) 778-5766

MASSACHUSETTS

Brimfield Antiques and Collectibles
Rt. 20
Brimfield, MA
*Held the first week of May, July, and
    September. Everything from large pieces
    of furniture to vintage textiles.*

Crafter's Potpourri
410 Alden Rd.
Fairhaven, MA 02719
(508) 997-4707
*Country gift shop featuring handcrafted
    works from New England artisans.*

Crate and Barrel
1045 Massachusetts Ave.
Cambridge, MA 02138
(617) 547-3994
*Specialty store featuring housewares,
    indoor/outdoor furniture, and
    storage items.*

Domain
7 Newbury St.
Boston, MA 02116
(617) 266-5252
and
The Mall at Chestnut Hill
Chestnut Hill, MA 02167
(617) 964-6666
*Home furnishings and decorative
    accessories from around the world.*

La Ruche
168 Newbury St.
Boston, MA 02116
(617) 536-6366
*Handpainted furniture, linens, tableware,
 mohair throws, and decorative
 accessories all with a touch
 of whimsy.*

Leonard's Antiques, Inc.
600 Taunton Ave.
Seekonk, MA 02771
(508) 336-8585
*Hundreds of antique post beds; also, rough
 and finished period antique furniture.*

London Lace
215 Newbury St.
Boston, MA 02116
(617) 267-3506
*Lace window coverings, antique lace
 linens, and yardage.*

Marcoz Antiques
177 Newbury St.
Boston, MA 02116
(617) 262-0780
*Antique French, English, and American
 decorative furnishings and accessories.*

Pinch Pottery/Ferrin Gallery
179 Main St.
Northampton, MA 01060
(413) 586-4509
*Functional decorative, and
 architectural ceramics.*

Renovator's Supply Co.
Renovator's Old Mill
Miller's Falls, MA 01349
(413) 659-2241
Period brass lighting. Catalog.

Salmon Falls Artisans Showroom
Box 176, Ashfield St.
Shelburne Falls, MA 01370
(413) 625-9883
*Gallery representing 200 of the
 region's craftspeople.*

Shaker Workshops
P.O. Box 1028
Concord, MA 01742
*Baskets in the Shaker style. Also trays,
 containers, boxes.*

Yankee Candle Co.
Rt. 5
South Deerfield, MA 01373
(413) 665-8306
*Tapers, tumblers, pillars, tealights
 in a variety of scents and sizes.
 Wholesale/retail.*

MICHIGAN

Lloyd/Flanders Industries
3010 Tenth St.
P.O. Box 500
Menominee, MI 49858
(800) 526-9894
Indoor/outdoor wicker furniture.

Village Green Antiques
8023 Church St., Box 159
Richland, MI 49083
(616) 629-4268
Antique period and country furniture and
accessories, period and folk paintings,
and English and Chinese export
porcelain.

Watch Hill Antiques and Interiors
330 E. Maple Rd.
Birmingham, MI 48009
(248) 644-7445
European country antique and custom
pine furniture including painted
furniture, tables and chairs, and
armoires.

MINNESOTA

Christopher Blake
16296 Elm Way
Belle Plaine, MN 56011
Featuring birdhouses, folk art, garden
accents, and furniture.

MISSISSIPPI

Bobbie King Antiques
Woodland Hills Shopping Center
667 Duling Ave.
Jackson, MS 39216
(601) 362-9803
Antique American furniture, vintage
linens and textiles, and beds.

The Mississippi Crafts Center
Natchez Trace Pkwy, Box 69
Ridgeland, MS 39158
(601) 856-7546
Crafts and folk art.

MISSOURI

Jack Parker Antiques and Fine Arts
4652 Shaw Ave.
Saint Louis, MO 63110
(314) 773-3320
Antique American country furniture,
American Indian art and artifacts.

The Picket Fence
211 E. 5th St.
Fulton, MO
(573) 642-2029
Specializing in primitive to European
giftware, antiques and crafts; most gift
and decor items are handmade and
handpainted.

NEBRASKA

From Nebraska Gift Shop
Historic Haymarket
140 N. 8th St.
Lincoln, NE 68508
(402) 476-2455
Specializing in Nebraska-made gift items,
including pottery, jewelry, gift baskets,
home decorating items, and much more.

NEW HAMPSHIRE

The League Gallery
205 N. Main St.
Concord, NH 03301
(603) 224-1471
Contemporary and traditional crafts.

Bert Savage Larch Lodge
Rt. 126
Center Strafford, NH 03815
(603) 269-7411
*Antique rustic furniture and accessories,
    antique canoes. By appointment only.*

Yield House
P.O. Box 5000
North Conway, NH 03860-5000
(800) 258-4720
Shaker design, benches, tables. Catalog.

NEW JERSEY

American By the Seashore
604 Broadway
Barnegat Light, NJ 08006
(609) 424-4781
*Country furniture, quilts and coverlets,
    marine art, folk carvings, and fish sets.*

The Sampler
96 Summit Avenue
Summit, NJ 07901
(908) 277-4747
*Decorative accessories for the home,
    including hand-painted objects
    and furniture.*

Union City Mirror and Table Co.
129 34th St., Box 825
Union City, NJ 07087
*Dressing Tables, mirrors, French
    provincial design. Wholesale.*

NEW MEXICO

Joshua Baer and Co.
116 1/2 E. Palace Ave.
Santa Fe, NM 87501
(505) 275-5630
*Southwestern furniture, Nineteenth-
    century Navaho blankets, and
    classic American Indian art.*

Mariposa Gallery
113 Romero St. NW, Old Town
Albuquerque, NM 87104
(505) 842-9097
*New Mexican contemporary crafts and
    jewelry.*

Morning Star Gallery
513 Canyon Rd.
Santa Fe, NM 87501
(505) 982-8187
American Indian Art.

Robert F. Nichols
419 Canyon Rd.
Santa Fe, NM 87501
(505) 982-2145
Contemporary Indian pottery.

Onorato
109 E. Palace Ave.
Santa Fe, NM 87501
(505) 983-7490
Specializing in wooden furniture.

Jonathan Parks/Julie Vaughan
Antique associates of Santa Fe
839 Paseo de Peralta, Suite M
Santa Fe, NM 87501
(505) 982-1446
*Country antiques and American
    Indian Art.*

NEW YORK CITY

ABC Carpet & Home
888 Broadway
New York, NY 10003
(212) 473-3000
*Huge selection of old and new items,
    including accessories.*

America Hurrah
766 Madison Ave.
New York, NY 10021
(212) 535-1930
*Antiques, including quilts, American
    folk art, and Native American Art.*

American Craft Museum Shop
40 W. 53rd St.
New York, NY 10019
(212) 956-6047
Items of all craft media.

Aphrodesia
264 Bleecker St.
New York, NY 10014
(212) 989-6440
Dried flowers, herbs, spices essential oils.

Betty Jane Bart Antiques
1225 Madison Ave.
New York, NY 10128
(212) 410-2702
*Early European furniture (some painted),
    mirrors and unique chandeliers.*

British Khaki Home Furnishings
214 W. 39th St.
New York, NY 10018
(212) 221-1199
*Variety of dressers, dressing tables.
    By appointment only.*

c.i.t.e
100 Wooster St.
New York, NY 10012
(212) 431-7272
*Antique chairs as well as other antique
    pieces.*

Claiborne Gallery
452 West Broadway
New York, NY 10012
(212) 475-3072
*Antique accessories, country furniture,
    iron furniture.*

Cobweb
116 W. Houston St.
New York, NY 10012
(212) 505-1558
Antique country and formal furniture
and decorative accessories from Brazil,
Morocco, Spain, Portugal, and the
Middle East.

Coming To America
276 Lafayette St.
New York, NY 10012
(212) 343-2968
Sofa and chairs designed by
David Drummond.

Country Flairs
15 E. 16th St.
New York, NY 10003
(212) 627-8300
Ceramic, teracotta, stone and mosaic
tile floor coverings.

Distant Origin
153 Mercer St.
New York, NY 10012
(212) 941-0024
Mexican Mennonite couches, sofas,
antique contemporary chairs.

Elizabeth Street Garden and Gallery
210 Elizabeth St.
New York, NY 10012
(212) 941-4800
Garden statues, gazebos, furniture,
fountains. Wholesale/retail.

Evergreen Antiques
1249 Third Ave.
New York, NY 10021
(212) 744-5664
Painted Scandinavian country furniture
with some pine pieces.

The Finished Room
1027 Lexington Avenue
New York, NY 10021
(212) 717-7626
Small furniture, pillows, decorative
accessories.

Laura Fisher Antiques
1050 Second Ave., Gallery #84
New York, NY 10022
(212) 838-2596
Antique American quilts, hooked rugs,
coverlets, American folk art, and
other textiles.

Gordon Foster, Ltd.
1322 Third Ave.
New York, NY 10021
(212) 744-4922
Antique baskets and home accessories.

Henro
525 Broome St.
New York, NY 10013
(212) 343-0221
Primitive antique furniture, old toys,
McCoy Pottery, Bauer pottery,
silver hotel plates.

Hinton & Company
108 Wooster St.
New York, NY 10012
(212) 343-2430
Contemporary collectibles, gift items, antiques.

Hometown
131 Wooster St.
New York, NY 10012
(212) 674-5770
American antiques.

Howard Kaplan Antiques
827 Broadway
New York, NY 10003
(212) 674-1000
French country designs.

Leo Design
413 Bleecker Street
New York, NY 10014
(212) 929-8466
Period and reproduction Arts & Crafts pieces and decorative items.

Leron
750 Madison Ave.
New York, NY 10021-7009
(800) 9linen9 (954-6369)
Elegant embroidered bed linens.

Adrien Linford
927 Madison Ave.
New York, NY 10021
(212) 628-4500
Home accessories, tabletop, bowls and gift items.

Lexington Gardens
1011 Lexington Ave
New York, NY 10021
(212) 861-4390
Contemporary wares and antique furniture; popular with New York designers.

Regis, Ltd.
68 Thompson St.
New York, NY 10012
(212) 334-2110
Antiques and decorative objects.

Steve Miller American Folk Art
17 E. 96th St.
New York, NY 10028
(212) 348-5219
Specializing in antique weather vanes, primitive paintings, and folk sculpture.

Judith and James Milne, Inc.
506 E. 74th St.
New York, NY 10021
(212) 472-0107 weekdays
(914) 255-8660 weekends
American county antiques and quilts.

Susan Parrish Antiques
390 Bleecker St.
New York, NY 10014
(212) 645-5020
Early-nineteenth-century painted furniture, folk art, Navaho rugs, and Indian artifacts, as well as antique quilts and linens.

Pierre Deux
870 Madison Ave.
New York, NY 10021
(212) 570-9343
and
369 and 381 Bleecker St.
New York, NY 10014
(212) 243-7740
French country home furnishings and
traditional fabrics. The shop at Bleecker
St. features French country antiques.

Portico Bed & Bath
139 Spring St.
New York, NY 10012
(212) 343-2230
Wrought-iron, cast-iron beds, plus linens.

San Lorenzo
123 West Broadway
New York, NY 10013
(212) 766-4770
A mix of European furniture, modern art,
and eclectic decorative accessories.

Pam Scurry's Wicker Garden
1318 Madison Ave.
New York, NY 10128
(212) 410-7000
Victorian antique wicker, antique brass
and iron beds, vintage linens, and
children's furniture.

Barton Sharpe, Ltd.
119 Spring St.
New York, NY 10012
(212) 925-9562
Windsor, Chippendale, and Queen Anne
chairs.

George Smith Sofas and Chairs
73 Spring St.
New York, NY 10012
(212) 226-4747
Handmade English furniture.
Wholesale/retail.

Stickley
160 5th Ave.
New York, NY 10010
(212) 337-0700
Gustav Stickley's American arts and crafts
and mission furniture still in production
by the original manufacturer.

The Store Next Door
943 Madison Ave.
New York, NY 10021
(212) 606-0200
The Whitney Musuem's showcase shop
for American furniture and collectibles.

Wolfman Gold & Good, Inc.
117 Mercer St.
New York, NY 10012
(212) 431-1888
Old and new accessories, including
flatware. No catalog.

The Works Gallery
1250 Madison Ave.
New York, NY 10128
(212) 996-0300
Crafts made by artisans countrywide.

Zona
97 Green St.
New York, NY 10012
(212) 925-6750
*Furniture of the Southwest, gardening
tools, life-style accessories, and
found objects.*

NEW YORK STATE

Balasses House Antiques
Main Street & Hedges Lane
Amagansett, NY 11930
(516) 267-3032
Antique country furniture and accessories.

C. & W. Mercantile
Main St.
Bridgehampton, NY 11932
(516) 537-7914
*Linens, rugs, baskets, and decorative
objects.*
The cotton throw found on p. 133 comes
from this store.

Casa el Patio
38 Newtown Lane
Easthampton, NY 11937
(516) 329-0300
*McCoy pottery, candles, antique painted
furniture and accessories.*

Country Living
26 Montauk Hwy
East Hampton, NY 11937
(516) 324-7371
*Old and new folk art, furniture, and
lamps.*

Suzanne Courcier/Robert Wilkins
11463 Rt. 223
Austerlitz, NY 12017
(518) 392-5754
*American antiques, Shaker pieces, and
paint-decorated items.*

Fisher's Main Street
Sag Harbor, NY 11963
(516) 725-0006
*Antique stripped pine and country
furnishings, quilts and pottery.*

Gaglio & Molnar, Inc.
Box 375
Wurtsboro, NY 12790
(914) 888-5077
*Antiques, furniture, accessories, American
folk art. By appointment only.*

Morgan MacWhinnie
American Antiques
520 North Sea Rd.
Southampton, NY 11968
(516) 283-3366
*American eighteenth- and nineteenth-
century formal and country furniture.*

Meyda Tiffany
1123 Stark St.
Utica, NY 13502
(315) 797-8775

New Budoff Corporation
East Broadway, P.O. Box 530
Monticello, NY 12701
(800) 548-0204
*Solid-oak Adirondack furniture.
Wholesale.*

Only Yesterday
608 Warren St.
Hudson, NY 12534
(518) 828-6824
Saturdays only
*An eclectic mix of "classics from the
    1860's to the 1960's" which includes
    Victoriana, country items, rock 'n' roll
    memorabilia, china, vintage linens,
    Art Deco items, and jewelry.*

Pritam & Eames
27–29 Race Lane
East Hampton, NY 11937
(516) 324-7111
*Original furniture, ceramics, metal,
    and glass objects.*

Gene Reed/A Country Gallery
75 S. Broadway
Nyack, NY 10960
(914) 358-3750
*Primitive furniture, newly crafted folk art,
    and gift items.*

John Keith Russell Antiques
Spring St.
South Salem, NY 10590
(914) 763-8144
*Rare and unusual American furniture,
    plus Shaker pieces and decorative arts.*

Summerhouse Antiques
70 Main St
Southampton, NY 11968
(516) 287-1800
*Featuring the Ralph Lauren Home
    Collection.*

Wonderful Things
Rte. 66 at Shaker Museum Rd.
Malden Bridge, NY 12115
(518) 766-4650
*Eighteenth-century American and
    Continental furniture and decorations,
    folk art, and American Indian art.*

Wood Classics, Inc.
Osprey Lane
Gardiner, NY 12525
(914) 255-5599
*Teak and mahogany tables and chairs,
    planters, mission furniture, and British,
    Chippendale, and Georgian benches.*

NORTH CAROLINA

Edgar B.
P.O. Box 849, 3550 Highway 158
Clemmons, NC 27012
(800) 628-3808
*Represents over 200 furniture
    manufacturers. Catalog.*

Broyhill Furniture Industries
1 Broyhill Park
Lenoir, NC 28633
(704) 758-3111
*Modern, contemporary, country,
    Southwestern design. Wholesale.*

Cameroon's
University Mall
Chapel Hill, NC 27514
(919) 942-5554
Original art, ceramics, and clay.

Hillary's, Ltd.
1669 North Market Sq.
Raleigh, NC 27609
(919) 878-6633
*Formal and country English and
    American Furniture.*

Lexington Furniture Company
P.O. Box 1008
Lexington, NC 27293
(704) 249-5300
*Carries Mary Emmerling's "American
    Country West" furniture. Wholesale.*

Traditions Pottery
4443 Bolick Rd.
Lenoir, NC 28645
(828) 295-6416
*Sixth generation potter makes folk art
    pottery, pitchers, candlesticks,
    and teapots.*

Marion Travis
P.O. Box 1041
Statesville, NC 28687
(704) 528-4424
Ladder-back chairs in a variety of styles.

OHIO

Antiques in the Bank
3500 Loraine Ave.
Cleveland, OH 44113
(216) 281-7440
*Architectural artifacts, antique furniture,
    and decorative accessories.*

Federation Antiques
2124 Madison Rd.
Cincinnati, OH 45208
(513) 321-2671
*Antique American quilts and folk art,
    and English and American period and
    country furniture.*

Oh Suzanna
16 S. Broadway
Lebanon, OH 45036
(513) 932-8246
American antiques, quilts, and textiles.

Thru the Grapevine
3149 State Route 133, P.O. Box 250
Bethel, OH 45106
(513) 734-2710
*Baskets, grapevine wreaths.
    Wholesale/retail.*

PENNSYLVANIA

Amish Country Collection
RD 5, Sunset Valley Road
Newcastle, PA 16105
(412) 458-4811
*Handpainted, custom-designed, hickory-
    branch mirrors. Wholesale/retail.*

Helen Drutt Gallery
1721 Walnut St.
Philadelphia, PA 19103
(215) 735-1625
Ceramics, jewelry, textiles, and furniture.

M. Finkel & Daughter
936 Pine St.
Philadelphia, PA 19107
(215) 627-7797
Period furniture (primarily country),
  painted pieces, needlework, quilts,
  folk art.

Gargoyles Ltd.
512 S. Third St.
Philadelphia, PA 19147
(215) 629-1700
Architectural artifacts, accessories, and
  antique and reproduction furniture.

Lewis Keister Antiques
209 Market St.
Lewisburg, PA 17837
(717) 523-3945
Textiles, quilts, accessories.
  Wholesale/retail.

Meetinghouse Antique Shop
509 Bethlehem Pike
Fort Washington, PA 19034
(215) 646-5126
Period and country antique furniture
  and accessories.

Olde Hope Antiques
Box 209, Route 202
New Hope, PA 18938
(215) 862-5055
Painted and decorated Pennsylvania
  furniture, folk paintings, vanes, textiles,
  and related accessories.

Rittenhouse Gift & Home
1714 Locust Street
Philadelphia, PA 19103
(215) 545-4915
Painted furniture and a wide range of
  decorative accessories.

Linda and Howard Stein
Rt. 202, P.O. Box 11
Lahaska, PA 18931
(215) 297-0606
Antiques decorative accessories, folk art.
  Wholesale/retail.

Union City Chair Company
18 Market St.
Union City, PA 16438
(814) 438-3878
Wood chairs in various styles and sizes.
  Wholesale.

The Works Gallery
319 South St.
Philadelphia, PA 19147
(215) 922-7775
Crafts made by artisans countrywide.

RHODE ISLAND

Askam and Telham, Inc.
12 Main St.
Wickford, RI 02852
(401) 295-0891
*Home Accessories, including needlepoint
and other pillows, reproduction antique
bird cages, and mohair throws.*

TEXAS

American Folk Arts
P.O. Box 11131
Spring, TX 77391-1131
(713) 712-8308
*Specializing in cloth dolls, quilts, cross
stitch patterns, painted wood collectibles,
and patterns for dolls and quilts.*

Eclectic Ethnographic Arts Gallery
700 N. Lamar St.
Austin, TX 78703
(512) 477-1863

The Galveston Arts Center
2127 Strand
Galveston, TX 77550
(409) 763-2403
*Three galleries encompassing
contemporary regional artists and
their decorative objects.*

Jabberwocky
207 E. Main Street
Fredericksburg, TX 78624
(830) 997-7071
*Quilts and antique linens; also small
folk art objects.*

Made in France
2913 Fernadale Pl.
Houston, TX 77098
(713) 529-7949
*French country antiques, new rush-seat
chairs, and handpainted lamps.*

Martinek Designs
4535 Travis at Knox
Dallas, TX 75205
(800) 852-9712
*Hand-carved, hand-crafted, country
French designs. Wholesale.*

Pier 1 Imports
P.O. Box 962030
Fort Worth, TX 76161-0020
(800) 447-4371
*Bowls, baskets, home furnishings and
accessories. Catalog.*

Room Service by Ann Fox
4354 Lover's Lane
Dallas, TX 75225
(214) 369-7666
*Antique beds, great new fabrics,
paintings, vintage memorabilia.*

Surroundings
1710 Sunset Blvd.
Houston, TX 77005
(713) 527-9838
*Specializing in Indonesian and Mexican
furniture; Also, pots and dishes.*

VERMONT

Bennington Potters
324 Country St.
Bennington, VT 05201
Traditional-style earthenware, including
  spatterware.

Sweet Cecily
42 Main St.
Middlebury, VT 05753
(802) 388-3353
Located in an old ice cream parlor, this
  store specializes in folk arts and crafts,
  including pottery, weaving, and boxes.

Vermont State Craft Center at
  Frog Hollow
Mill St.
Middlebury, VT 05753
(802) 388-3177
American craft items, many made by
  Vermont craftspeople.

VIRGINIA

Brentwood Manor Furnishings
316 Virginia Ave.
Clarksville, VA 23927
(804) 374-4297
Variety of dressers, dressing tables, mirrors.

Chadwick's
5805 Grove Avenue
Richmond, VA 23226
(804) 285-3355
A full range of decorative items for the
  home.

Colonial Williamsburg Foundation
Dept 023, P.O. Box 3532
Williamsburg, VA 23187-3532
(800) 446-9240
Colonial-style home accessories, from
  glass hurricane lamps to checked
  blankets. Mail order. Catalog.

Crate in Motion Furniture
3605 Virginia Beach Blvd.
Virginia Beach, VA 23452
(804) 431-1333
Solid-wood dressers and chests of drawers.

The Lane Company, Inc.
East Franklin Ave., P.O. Box 151
Altavista, VA 24517
(804) 369-5641
Country collections, lacquer, contemporary.
  Wholesale.

Paper Plus
5804 Grove Avenue
Richmond, VA 23226
(804) 288-2662
Vintage and needlepoint pillows, woven rugs,
  pottery, and other decorative accessories.

Random Harvest
810 King St.
Old Town
Alexandria, VA 22314
(703) 548-8820
Vintage furniture (ready for upholstery),
  textiles, and related decorative objects.

WASHINGTON

The Best of All Worlds
523 Union St.
Seattle, WA 98101
(206) 623-2525
Gifts and decorative accessories.

Flying Shuttle
607 First Ave.
Seattle, WA 98104
(206) 343-9762
Interior Accessories and other craft art.

David Reed Weatherford—
   Antiques and Interiors
133 14th Ave. E
Seattle, WA 98112
(206) 329-6533
*Eighteenth- and nineteenth-century
   furniture; also, fine art and
   decorative accessories.*

WISCONSIN

Rowe Pottery Works
404 England St.
Cambridge, WI 53523-9116
(800) 356-5003
*Salt-glazed stoneware; also, iron racks,
   pan stands and trivets, and candle-
   holders. Mail order service available.*

INDEX